THE BUDDHIST LEGEND
OF
JIMUTAVAHANA
AND THE
NAGANANDA

THE BUDDHIST LEGEND OF JIMUTAVAHANA

FROM THE KATHA-SARIT-SAGARA
(THE OCEAN-RIVER OF STORY)
DRAMATIZED IN THE
NAGANANDA
(THE JOY OF THE WORLD OF SERPENTS)

A BUDDHIST DRAMA BY SRI HARSHA DEVA

TRANSLATED FROM THE SANSKRIT

B. HALE WORTHAM

ISBN : 978-93-5324-555-9 (HB)

First Published, London

Published, 2020

Published by

Facsimile Publisher
12 Pragati Market
Ashok Vihar, Ph-2
Delhi-110052
E-mail: books@facsimilepublisher.com

Printed at: G. Print Process, Delhi.

The Buddhist Legend of Jimutavahana

Author: B. Hale Worthama

THE BUDDHIST LEGEND OF JÎMÛTAVÂHANA

FROM THE KATHÂ-SARIT-SÂGARA
[THE OCEAN-RIVER OF STORY]

DRAMATIZED IN THE

NÂGÂNANDA
[THE JOY OF THE WORLD OF SERPENTS]

A BUDDHIST DRAMA BY ŚRÎ HARSHA DEVA

TRANSLATED FROM THE SANSKRIT

BY THE REVEREND

B. HALE WORTHAM, B.A.
TRIN. COLL., OXON.
RECTOR OF DUNTON WAYLETT

Translator of the Śatakas of Bhartrihari, the Hitopadeśa,
The Śuka Saptati (70 tales of a parrot), etc., etc.

LONDON
GEORGE ROUTLEDGE & SONS, LIMITED
NEW YORK: E. P. DUTTON & CO.

CONTENTS

INTRODUCTION

THE Buddhist legend of Jîmûtavâhana is related twice in the course of the Kathâsaritsâgara, in the 22nd and 90th chapters, and is dramatised in a play called the Nâgânanda. The first of these works, the title of which means the "Ocean-river of Story," is a production of the 10th or 11th century A.D. It is entirely in verse, founded by its author, Somadeva, on an earlier collection of existing legends related in a work called Vrihat Kathâ, which goes back to the 2nd century A.D. The drama, the Nâgânanda, follows the line of the legend very closely, as given in the 22nd chapter of the Kathâsaritsâgara. Nâgânanda signifies "The joy of the world of serpents," and refers to the hero Jîmûtavâhana, who is the centre of the drama. The authorship is uncertain, though all duly qualified judges assign the 7th century A.D. as the date of its composition. The editor of the drama in the original Sanskrit, published at Bombay in 1892, Śrinivas Govind Bhânap (from whose edition the following translation has been made) attributes it to King Śrî Harsha, and is of opinion that it is by the same author as a drama called the Ratnâvali. He justifies this by the similarity (or more than similarity) between certain expressions and situations in the two dramas, and which would be the most barefaced plagiarism, unless they were the work of the same author. Professor Cowell (the late learned Sanskrit professor at Cambridge), on the other hand, thinks that the difference of religious tone between the two dramas makes it quite impossible that they can be by the same author. Whoever might have been the real author, it is quite possible that the play was attributed to King Śrî Harsha, out of compliment to him, since it was brought out by his order and under his patronage, though he might have had nothing to do with its composition.

The interesting point about the drama is its religious atmosphere. It is a practical exposition of the doctrines and practices of Buddhism. The play itself is a mixture of Buddhism and Hindûism. It opens, as usual, with a benediction, but the benediction is addressed to the Buddha, and is in this respect unique. The worship of Gaûri, however, is represented as still existing, and the heroine pays homage to her in her temple. The hero is a confirmed Buddhist. He has apparently no leanings to Brâhmanism, and makes little or no reference to worship, sacrifice, or to any of the Hindû deities. His whole religious attitude is distinctly subjective. He lives under an entirely different religious condition from that of the other characters in the play. He is the exponent of a very exalted system of morality, which he puts into practice. At the same time he stands alone, and finds no sympathy for his tenets, in those by whom he is surrounded. In fact, it is pretty clear, as his wife's brother Mitrâvasu sees, that his doctrines, if carried into practice, must lead to political and social chaos. The drama finally concludes with the introduction of the goddess Gaurî, who displays her divine and miraculous power in raising the hero to life. In this particular conjunction the Buddhist Jîmûtavâhana does pay her something like worship : perhaps we may take it that while he does not think the national worship of any particular consequence, he has no objection to pay a certain amount of respect to the deities of his forefathers. The play, with its Buddhist and Hindû religious element running side by side, represents, perhaps, what existed (or what was intended to exist) under the liberal and tolerant rule of Śrî Harsha. The Buddhist and the Hindû agree to bury the feuds of a thousand years, and live together in peace and harmony, the beliefs and practices of each going on side by side.

The drama is highly sensational, and the characters are well worked out. The character on which the whole action turns, that of Jîmûtavâhana, is, of course, the most carefully elaborated. In fact, the whole interest of the drama centres on him, all the other characters being entirely subordinate. The subject would be an interesting one at any time or place, but to the audience who saw it for the first time it must have been absolutely entrancing, as emotional (to use the word in no invidious sense) as the Œdipus Rex of the Greek stage, or the Passion play at Ober-Ammergau. The editor of the Sanskrit original (to whom I have referred) thinks that the style of the drama (except in a few places) does not rise to the dignity of the subject, and is wanting in literary finish and grace, and that as a work of art it cannot be considered on a level with the great masterpieces of the Hindû stage. Be this as it may, and no doubt the editor is a very good judge, in spite of its deficiencies, the dignity of the subject itself must remain, nor could it altogether be destroyed, however imperfect its expression.

The character of Jîmûtavâhana (as has been said) is carefully drawn and is worth studying. In the beginning of the first act he is introduced to us, calmly setting forth his sentiments and his principles, founded on obedience to his father's will and self-renunciation. Next, he is shown us on his human side. Self-renunciation is clearly not a natural, but an acquired virtue. He is perfectly human both in his courtship and in the scene with Malayavatî, the princess whom he marries; and then, at last, after this episode, he comes before us again carrying out his principles to their farthest point and in their highest perfection. He has a human side, as well as a divine side, and the divine side is eventually victorious. The position of Jîmûtavâhana at the beginning of the drama is that which Buddhists call a " Bodhisat," one who has passed through all the births necessary to attain perfection but one, and the next birth is to place him on a level with the Supreme Buddha, and he will attain to Nirvana. In the case of Jîmûtavâhana this is not what happens, as we might have expected. His self-sacrifice ought to have brought him to Nirvana, but it does not. After his death he returns to earth in his former position, only much more glorious and magnificent, raised to life again by the famous Gaurî, the " Brilliant " goddess, the wife of Śiva, who stands at the head of the Hindû Pantheon. And here it seems as if we had an example of the compromise between Buddhism and Hindûism, and which, as I have already suggested, seems to be formulated by this drama.

The story, one of singular interest and beauty, is a strange echo from the world of Christianity. Not that I suggest the influence of Christianity, as might be supposed from the verse of St. John's Gospel which stands at the head of this book. Nor is it necessary to suppose anything of the kind.

All that need be said is, that there is a coincidence between certain lines of thought and action. The play is many centuries later than Christianity, though the legend is no doubt some centuries older. The truth is that we have here an exemplification of St. Paul's words, when he says, speaking of the Gentiles, that " He left not Himself without witness."

That the Buddha was a saint after his manner and in his own time is undoubted. We may go farther, and say that he would have been a saint at any time, or any place, in the world's history. The same Light and Spirit which led him as far as it did in the times when he lived, would no doubt have led him still farther if he had lived under the more perfect Revelation. His advanced morality and his spiritual enlightenment not only placed him far above all his fellows, but made him the founder of a great religious system; and his fame for sanctity has raised him to such an exalted position that, as some tell us, the Buddha has been enrolled under the name of " St. Josaphat " among the Saints of the Catholic Church.

THE STORY OF JÎMÛTAVÂHANA

(*Kathâ Sarit Sâgara*, Tarânga 22, Śloka 16)

A MOUNTAIN called the Snowclad on this earth
Uprears its mighty form, the chief of hills,
Father of Parvatî,—of Gaurî's spouse
The spiritual head. In that great mount,
The home of the Vidyâharas, once dwelt
Their lord, Jîmûtaketu. To his house
Belonged a 'wishing tree,' the legacy
Of his forefathers, from its nature called
'The giver of desire.' And so the king
One day approached that heaven-sent tree and
said,
In supplicating tones: 'O deity!
Who ever grantest all we ask or seek,
Give me, I pray thee, now, a virtuous son,
For I am childless.' 'King,' replied the tree,
'Thy prayer is granted, thou shalt have a son;
Within his mind shall dwell the memory
Of former births; he shall be liberal,
The lover of all creatures.' Then the king,
Filled with delight, in adoration bowed
Before the tree, and straightway to his Queen
Bore the glad tidings. Soon a son was born,
And to the boy the father gave the name

Jîmûtavâhana. As time went on
The youth increased in stature, while the love
Which filled his inmost nature, step by step,
Grew with his outward form. At last, the prince,
Proclaimed Successor to his father's crown,
Filled with compassion for all living things
That move upon this earth, in secret spoke,
And thus addressed his father, who with joy
Heard his son's words. 'Surely I know full well
That all things perish: nothing on the earth
Has an abiding place; one thing alone,—
The glory of the virtuous, replete
With purity,—though countless ages pass,
Shall never fail. If men of noble mind
Have gained renown by showering kindnesses
On others, more than life, far more than wealth,
They value that fair glory. As for us—
If our good fortune—our prosperity—
Be for ourselves alone, nor overflow
On the less fortunate, then like a flash
Of lightning shall our fortune pass away,
And vanish into air. This "Wishing tree"
Grants all that we desire; if, then, we pray
The tree to pour its blessings o'er the world,
Nor keep them selfishly,—then shall its fruit
Be ours indeed. So let me supplicate
The wishing tree that by its boundless wealth
The multitudes of men, who pass their lives
In poverty, may be relieved.' Thus spoke
Jîmûtavâhana: gladly his sire
Assented, and the youth invoked the tree.
'O Bounteous tree! The giver of all good

To us; fulfil this day our earnest prayer;
Banish from earth all want and poverty.
Hail to thee! friendly one! Thou hast been sent
To bless the world with wealth, therefore I pray
Bestow on men the wealth that they desire.'
In answer to Jîmûtavâhana
The self-denying one, the tree sent down
Gold in abundant showers on the earth,
While all mankind rejoiced. Who could have bent
The wishing tree to carry out his will
And rain down plenty, even though he were
Incarnate Wisdom, but the glorious
Jîmûtavâhana? Therefore to him
Were all the regions of the earth fast bound
By ties of gratitude, and o'er the heav'n
His spotless fame extended far and wide.

Then the relations of the King uprose,—
Even of King Jîmûtaketu,—full
Of hatred, since the throne was firmly fixed
By his son's glory; and their minds they set
To seize upon that place wherein the tree,
The giver of all blessings, grew,—a place
Unfortified, easy to be o'ercome.
Therefore they met together, fully bent
On war. Then said Jîmûtavâhana,
Calm and composed, 'Father! this life of ours
Is even as a bubble on the stream.
Why should we then desire prosperity?
For even as a lamp, whose tongue of flame
Flickers before the wind, so among men
Is fortune. Who could ever hope to gain

(If he were wise at least) prosperity
From other's harm or death ? I will not fight
With kinsmen ; I will rather leave my realm
And dwell within the forest. Let them be !
We will not slay these miserable men,
Our brothers and our kin.' His father said,
Firmly resolved in mind : 'I, too, my son !
Will go with you, for I am old and grey,
And how should love for power abide in me
Since thou, all young and vigorous, hast cast
Thy realm aside, as though it were but straw,
Through love and pity ?' Thus the King
    approved
Jîmûtavâhana's advice, and left
His realm, departing with his wife and son
To Mount Malaya. There the youth abode
Within a grove, the Siddha's dwelling-place,
Where trees of sandal shadowed o'er the brooks,
Making his father's life his chiefest care.
And while he sojourned there, the Siddha prince.
Mitrâvasu, accepted as a friend,
The youth, whose sister in a former birth
Had loved Jîmûtavâhana. He saw,
And filled with perfect wisdom knew again
The damsel he had loved. Their mutual glance,
Like the frail meshes of the net which holds
The captive deer, ensnared each other's souls.
  One day the Siddha prince, his countenance
Beaming with joy, in sudden thought addressed
Jîmûtavâhana, whom the three worlds
Adored : 'A younger sister dwells with me,
Called Malayavatî : to thee I give

The maiden ; O ! do not refuse my gift ! '
Then spoke Jîmûtavâhana, and said :
' Prince ! in a former birth she was my wife,
Thou too my friend, even as dear to me
As my own heart ; to me is given the power
Of calling back to mind births past and gone.'
Mitrâvasu replied : ' Tell me, I pray,
The story of thy former births, I long
To hear it.' And Jîmûtavâhana,
Loving towards all creatures, answerèd :
' Hear then my tale : Once in a former birth
As a Vidyâdhara, flying through space,
I passed Himâlaya, whose lofty peaks
Shone forth beneath me, and I was beheld
By Śiva, sporting with his spouse, The god
Enraged, because my towering flight
Bore me above him, with a curse pronounced
This sentence on me : " In the world of men
In mortal guise thou shalt be born : a wife
From the Vidyâdharas thou shalt obtain.
Thou shalt appoint thy son to occupy
Thy room, and then once more remembering
Thy former birth, thou shalt again be born
As a Vidyâdhara." Thus Śiva spoke,
Yet while he cursed, foretelling too the end
Of his Anathema, and disappeared.
Soon after, in a merchant's family
I entered human form, and lived the son
Of a rich trader in a city named
Vallabhî : Vasudatta was the name
Bestowed on me. Time passed ; to manhood grown,

My father sent me forth, a retinue
Of servants following, to some far land
To traffic. On my journey, I was seized
By robbers in a forest; stripped of all
My merchandise, they loaded me with chains
And dragged me to their village, to the shrine
Of Durgâ, where a silken banner waved,
Crimson and long, like to the very tongue
Of Death, all eagerness to lick the blood
Of living things. Then to Pulindaka,
Their chief, they brought me, who was worshipping
Before the goddess, that within her shrine
I might be offered as a sacrifice.
And when he saw me, lo! the Savara chief,
Though but a savage, felt his inmost heart
Melt with compassion: for a causeless love
Which seems to spring unbidden in the heart
Tells us of friendship in a former birth.
Thus was I saved from slaughter by the King,
Who, still intent upon the sacrifice,
Prepared to make the offering of himself,
And so complete the rite. But while he thought
Thereon, a voice from heaven said: "O king!
Hurt not thyself! Ask of me what thou wilt,
It shall be granted thee, for thou hast been
Approved of me." Then filled with joy the king
Replied: "Since thou, O goddess, hast approved
My deeds, what should I further need? but yet—
One thing I ask of thee: in births to come,
May love between me and the merchant's son
Ever remain unchanged." "It shall be so",

Answered the goddess. Then the Savara prince
Restored me to my home loaded with wealth.
My father, seeing that I had returned
From a far-distant land, the jaws of death
Barely escaped, held a great festival
To do me honour. Then I saw again
After some time had passed the Savara chief
Led in a prisoner before the king
For sentence and for punishment: his crime
The plunder of a caravan. Straightway
I told my father, and I prayed the king
To spare the Savara. So my prayer was heard
And with a mighty sum of gold I saved
The Savara chief from death. Thus I repaid
His benefits, and to my own abode
I brought him home, and long I tended him
With loving care. After a time he turned
Departing to his village, while his heart
Tender with love was fixed upon me still.
And then he roamed the earth, seeking a gift
Worthy the kindnesses which I had showed
Towards him. As he wandered here and there,
He saw a lake before him, on its banks
A woman riding on a lion, young
And beautiful. The Savara chief, amazed,
Thought thus within himself. " Who may this
be ?
Is she a mortal ? How then does she ride
Upon a lion ? Can she be divine ?
But if a goddess, how should such as I
Behold her ? Surely clad in human form
I see her as the merit which I gained

In former births. Oh! could I only win
Her for my friend in marriage,—then indeed
I should bestow on him a just reward
For all his benefits." The Savara chief,
Thus thinking in himself, respectfully
Advanced to greet the maiden, who returned
His salutation. "Who art thou?" she said.
"Why hast thou come to this far-distant land?"
"I am a Savara prince," he made reply,
"Lo! I am seeking treasure in this wood,
And at the sight of thee I called to mind
The friend who saved my life, the merchant's son.
Matchless is he in youth and comeliness,
A very fount of nectar to the world,
Even as thou art. Fortunate the lot
Of that fair maid who shall bestow her hand
On one so full of generosity,
So full of love, of patience, of compassion.
If this surpassing lovely form of thine
Should fail of such a destiny, Alas!
Then Kâma bears indeed his bow in vain."
The maiden's mind by these enticing words
Was borne away, as though the spells of love
Bewildered her. "Where is this friend of thine?"
She said, under love's prompting, "Bring him here!
That I may see him." "Even so," replied
The Savara prince, and full of joy returned
To seek his friend, thinking his object gained.

Then bringing with him treasures—pearls and
musk,
He came to our abode, and entering in,
While all our house saluted him, he gave
My sire the present, worth a mighty sum
Of gold. After the day and following night
Had passed in feasting, then the Savara prince
Took me aside, and told me privately
The story of the maiden; and to me,
Full of excitement at the tale, he said,
"Come there with me, my friend!" When
nightfall came,
The Savara chief departed, bearing me
Along with him. And when the morning light
Shone forth, my father knew that I had gone
Together with the Savara prince; but yet,
Confiding in the prince's love for me,
He felt no grief. And I, as time went on,
Journeyed towards Himâlaya; the prince
Tending me on the way with loving care.
At length, one evening, we beheld the lake
Before our eyes, and in the forest bounds
We tarried all that night, eating the fruits
Which grew within the wood,—that lovely wood
Wherein the ground was strewed with creeper
flowers,
While all the air resounded with the hum
Of bees; sweet gentle breezes blew,—the herbs
Sent forth a gleaming light even like lamps.
And then all night we rested in that wood—
The chamber of delight. Next day the maid,
Riding upon the lion, like the moon

Resting upon an autumn cloud, drew near.
As she approached, my mind at every step
Flew as it were to meet her, and the prince,
Advancing tow'rds her, said in courteous tones :
" Goddess ! I offer thee my dearest friend,
Accept him as thy bridegroom." " Bring thy friend
Hither ", she answered, and with eyes of love
She glanced at me approaching her, and said,
" This friend of thine must surely be a god !
No mortal has so beautiful a form."
" Fair one ! I am a mortal ", I replied.
" A merchant's son, who dwells in Vallabhî.
My father by the favour of the god
Who wears upon his head the crescent moon
Received me as his son." Then said the maid,
Her eyes cast down through modesty, " The god
Hath now fulfilled his promise ; for he deigned
To tell me in a dream, ' To-morrow's sun
Shall show thy spouse to thee.' Lo ! here I find
In thee my husband," Thus she charmed my mind
With speech of nectar sweetness. Then the wood
We quitted, journeying homewards that the rites
Of marriage might be duly solemnized ;
And mounted on the lion, in my arms
Holding the maiden, we reached Vallabhî.
Then lo ! with wonder filled, the people ran
To tell my father ; marvelling, he came
To greet me. When he saw the gracefulness

And beauty of the maiden, and perceived
How fitly I had chosen her, his heart
Rejoiced, and to our marriage feast he called
Our friends and relatives. Thus she became
My spouse, and all my life was filled with peace
And happiness, blessed with a virtuous wife.
At length, as time went by, old age crept on,
And I, feeling disgust for earthly things
And weariness of life, I made my son
The ruler of my house, and then I turned,
Away, leaving domestic cares, and went
Into the forest. There intense desire
To leave this mortal frame possessed my mind.
Therefore I fixed my thought on things divine,
And from the mountain side I threw myself
Down headlong. So I quitted life. Now born
Again into the world, thou seest me
Jîmûtavâhana. To me belongs
The recollection of my former births.
Mitrâvasu thou art the Savara prince,
And this thy sister, Malayavatî,
Is that same damsel born again, whom I,
The merchant's son, chose in my former birth
To be my bride. Therefore 'tis right and good
That I should marry her. First do thou go
And tell my parents: then will I accept
Thy gift.' And when Mitrâvasu had heard
The story of Jîmûtavâhana,
He told his parents, who were filled with joy,
And gave their daughter Malayavatî
In marriage to Jîmûtavâhana,
And the pair dwelt in great prosperity

And happiness upon Malaya's mount.
  Once on a time Jîmûtavâhana
Was wandering amid the woods that gird
The shore ; and in that place he saw a man
Fearful and trembling ; and with loud lament
His mother followed, while the man would turn
And bid his mother leave him, but with tears
She never ceased to follow him. Behind
The pair there followed one in soldier's garb,
Who led the man up to a lofty rock
And left him. Then Jîmûtavâhana
Spoke to the man and said, 'Tell me, I pray,
Who art thou ? Why does this thy mother weep
For thee.' Then said the man, 'In bygone times
Kadrû and Vinatâ, Kâsyapa's wives,
Held a dispute. The horses of the sun
Were black', so one declared,—the other said
That they were white. The one who erred should
      serve
The other as a slave. Thus each agreed.
The subtle-minded Kadrû, fully bent
On victory, induced her sons the snakes
To send forth showers of venom o'er the steeds ;
And then she showed them all defiled and black
To Vinatâ. So by an artifice
Was Vinatâ o'ercome and made a slave.
How terrible is woman's spite which wreaks
Vengeance upon its kind. Then came the son
Of Vinatâ, Garuḍa, and he begged
His mother. Then the sons of Kadrû said,
" Garuḍa ! lo ! the gods have now begun
To churn the sea of milk. If thou wilt bring

The nectar from that sea, O mighty chief,
And give it us, thou shalt indeed redeem
Thy mother from her bonds of slavery."
Then to the sea of milk Garuḍa went,
And showed his mighty power, if by that means
He might obtain the nectar. Vishnu, pleased
With that display of might, exclaimed " Indeed
Thou hast delighted me! Ask what thou wilt,
And I will give it thee." Garuḍa, wroth,
Because his mother had been made a slave,
Replied, " I pray thee may the snakes become
My food." The god assented. So he gained
The nectar by his valour, and a boon
From Vishnu. As Garuḍa turned to go,
There met him Indra. " King of birds!" he said,
" I know thine errand; may thy power and might
Restrain these foolish snakes lest they consume
The nectar, and enable me to take
It from them." When Garuḍa heard these words,
He willingly complied, and to the snakes
Bearing the nectar in his hand he went,
Rejoicing in the thought of Vishṇu's boon;
Then standing at a distance, he addressed
The snakes, filled with alarm at Vishnu's gift:—
" Here is the nectar, lo! I bring it you,
Take it,—release my mother; if you fear
My power, I will place it on a bed
Of Darbha grass; and when you have restored
My mother I will go, and you can take

The nectar thence." All willingly the snakes
Assented, and upon a sacred bed
Of Kuśa grass, Garuḍa placed the bowl
Of nectar, and departed, having freed
His mother. Then the snakes approached to
taste
The nectar, but with sudden swoop from heaven
The mighty Indra fell, and bore away
The nectar from its bed of Darbha grass.
Then in despair the serpents licked the grass,
One single drop of nectar may remain
(They thought) upon the grass ; and thus their
tongues
Were split, and they became all double-tongued,
Nor gainéd aught. What can the greedy hope
To gain but ridicule ? And so the snakes
Failed to obtain the nectar, while their foe,
Garuḍa, fell upon them, and began,
Strong in the gift of Vishnu, to devour
Them up. And all the snakes in Pâtâla
Were dead with fear, the females cast their
young,
Over the serpent race destruction seemed
To hang. Then Vâsuki, the serpent King,
Seeing his enemy come day by day,
Foresaw the ruin of the serpent world,
And as a suppliant to Garuḍa said :
"O mighty one ! whose power and majesty
Are past resisting, as each day goes by
One serpent will I send thee, king of birds,
And on that sandy hill, hard by the sea,
My offering shalt thou find : nor enter thou

Pâtâla day by day, destroying all
The serpent race ; for then thy life
Will lose its object." Thus spoke Vâsuki.
Garuḍa to his words assented. In this place
Each day he eats the snake Vâsuki sends.
So have innumerable serpents met
Their death. I am a serpent too. My name
Is Śankachûḍa, and my time is come
To furnish forth a meal. The serpent King
Has therefore sent me to this rock of death,
Whither my mother follows me with tears
And lamentations sore.' Then grief possessed
Jîmûtavâhana, and thus he spoke :
'Ah ! but a coward is that king of thine !
He offers to his enemy as food
The people of his realm ! Why did he not
First offer up himself ? Oh, base thy King !
Since he the overthrow of all his race
Unmoved can witness. Ah ! how great a sin !
Garuḍa too commits. Lo ! mighty sins
Do even mighty men commit, impelled
By selfish greediness. Cheer up, my friend !
I will deliver thee, surrendering
My body to Garuḍa.' 'Mighty one !'
Responded Śankachûda ; 'This be far
From thee ! Thou wouldest not destroy a gem
To save a bit of glass. Never will I
Endure that foul disgrace through me should
fall
Upon my race.' Thus tried he to dissuade
Jîmûtavâhana, and to the shrine
Of Śiva went, thinking his time was come,

To offer adoration to the god.
And then indeed Jîmûtavâhana,
Of pity and compassion, as it were,
The very treasure house—thought that the chance
Had come, by offering of himself, to save
The serpent's life. Therefore he quickly sent
Mitrâvasu away, on some pretence.
Then came Garuḍa, and immediately
The earth began to tremble at the wind
Of his advancing wings, as though it shook
In wonder at the steadfast bravery
Of the great-minded one. Then rose in haste
Jîmûtavâhana, and filled with love
For living things, mounted upon the rock
Of death, knowing the quaking earth foretold
The advent of Garuḍa. Then swooped down
The serpent's enemy—the heavens grew dark
At his dread shadow, and he bore away
Jîmûtavâhana, while drops of blood
Flowed from the hero, and his jewelled crest
Fell to the ground, torn by Garuḍa's beak.
And flying to the topmost mountain peak,
The king of birds began to eat his prey.
Then instantly there fell from heaven a rain
Of flowers, while Garuḍa at the sight
Was filled with wonder. Soon this snake returned
Fresh from Gokarṇa's shrine, and when he saw
The rock of death wet with the drops of blood,
' Surely the mighty-minded one, (he thought)
Has offered up his life to ransom mine.

Oh, whither has Garuḍa borne him hence?
Lo! I will search for him, it may so chance
That I may find him.' Following the track
Left by the drops of blood, the serpent went.
Meanwhile Garuḍa with amazement saw
That gladness filled Jîmûtavâhana.
He ceased to eat him, and within himself
He thought: 'Who can this be? This must be one
To whom I have no right; for misery
Has no abode within his constant mind.
Lo! he rejoices in his fate!' Then said
Jîmûtavâhana, upon his aim
Intent: 'O King of birds! there still remains
Within my body flesh and blood: I pray
Why hast thou ceased to feed upon my form,
Seeing thy hunger is not satisfied?'
Filled with astonishment, the King of birds
Ceased from his meal, and said 'O! mighty one!
Surely thou art no snake; I pray thee, say,
Who art thou?' Then Jîmûtavâhana
(His answer just begun: 'I am a snake!
Eat me, I pray, for men of constant mind
With perseverance carry through the task
They have in hand'), heard from afar the voice
Of Śankachûḍa, 'King of birds! desist!
I am the snake prepared for thee! Alas!
How camest thou in recklessness and haste
To err so grievously?' Confusion seized
Garuḍa, and Jîmûtavâhana
Was overcome with grief, for his desire
Had fled, all unfulfilled. At last the truth

Was clear before Garuḍa, and he knew
His prey was not a serpent, but the king
Of the Vidyâdharas. Then deepest pain
Possessed his mind. 'Alas! my cruelty!'
He said; 'What sin has that brought forth in me!
How easily does sin lay hold on those
Who follow after sin! This noble one
Who for another's good has sacrificed
Himself, despising this illusive world,
Nor fears my power—all honour be to him,
And praise unceasing!' Then the king of birds,
To purify himself, into the flames
Was rushing headlong. 'King of birds', exclaimed
Jîmûtavâhana, 'Do not despair!
If thou wouldst truly turn from guilt—repent!
Slay no more serpents for thy food—repent
Of those which thou didst eat in times gone by;
So shalt thou find a remedy for guilt,
None other may avail.' The king of birds
Heard and rejoiced, determined to repent,
Obedient to Jîmûtavâhana
As to a ghostly father. Then to heaven
He went to bring down nectar, to revive
The wounded prince, and to restore to life
The serpents who had perished, and whose bones
Alone were left. Then Gaurî came from heaven
In human form, and on the mighty one
She poured forth showers of nectar: and his limbs,

Renewed in greater beauty than before,
Were given back to him, while through the sky
The heavenly music rang, and all the gods
Rejoiced. Garuḍa, too, returned from heaven,
Bearing the nectar; and along the shore
He sprinkled the life-giving drops. And lo!
The serpents that had perished, once again
Rose up, clothed with the forms that they had worn
In life, and filled that forest by the shore—
Crowds upon crowds of serpents pressing on;—
It seemed even as though the serpent world,
Forgetting their dread enemy, had come
To see and honour their deliverer.
And round Jîmûtavâhana his friends,
His wife, his parents, clustered, and they praised
Him for his glory, and undying fame.
Could aught but triumph reign in word or thought
Since joy had banished pain. Then to his home,
Together with his wife, and friend, and son,
Jîmûtavâhana, compassionate
Towards all living things, departing, reigned
The sovereign lord of the Vidyâdharas.

NÂGÂNANDA

DRAMATIS PERSONÆ

JÎMÛTAVÂHANA : Prince of the Vidyâdharas.

JÎMÛTAKETU : King of the Vidyâdharas, father to Jîmûtavâhana.

VIŚVÂVASU : King of the Siddhas.

MITRÂVASU : Son of Viśvâvasu.

ŚANKHACHÛDA : Prince of the Nâgâs.

GARUḌA : King of the Birds.

ÂTREYA : a Brâhman, the King's confidant (The Vidûshaka).

SEKHARAKA : a hanger-on.

THE MESSENGER.

THE CHAMBERLAIN.

THE GODDESS, GAURÎ.

THE QUEEN OF THE VIDYÂDHARAS : Mother to Jîmûtavâhana.

MALAYAVATÎ : daughter to Viśvâvasu.

CHATURIKÂ : her attendant.

SANKHACHÛDA'S MOTHER.

FEMALE ATTENDANTS.

NÂGÂNANDA

ACT I

(*Opening Benediction*)

' On whom dost thou pretend to meditate,—
Thine eyes fast closed ? Just for one moment
gaze
On us, afflicted through the shafts of love.
Ah ! Thou art called a saviour ! 'Tis a name
To which thou hast no right: for thou art
false.
Thou hast no pity. Ah ! What cruelty
Can equal thine ? '
May the enlightened one
The conqueror, addressed by Mara's nymphs
In jealous wrath, protect you ! May the lord
Of all the ancient sages be your guard !
For he, tempted by Kâma with his bow
Drawn to the full—tempted in frantic dance
By Kâmá's followers with resounding drums,—
Tempted by Siddhas too, with heads bent low
In homage—by the Nymphs with quivering eyes
From which shot forth the glance of wrath, or
scorn,
Or jest :—Yet he, with heavenly wisdom filled,
And wrapped in meditation, cast aside

Their wiles, while Indra gazed, in wonder lost,
To see such constancy.

End of Benediction.

Enter JÎMÛTAVÂHANA *and* ÂTREYA.

JÎMÛT. My dearest friend! Youth is indeed the time
Wherein the fruit is gained of all delights,
'Twixt right and wrong it knows no difference.
A time to be despised! but yet perchance
Ev'n from this hated time, if I subserve
My parents' will in all things, I may gain
Some profit.

ÂTREYA (*angrily*). No wonder you are so unhappy! Here you are devoting yourself to two old people, who are as good as dead! What's the use of it all? Now take my advice. Give up all this slavery, and enjoy all the pleasures of sovereignty as you ought!

JÎMÛT. My friend! You speak not well.
What glory is there in a monarch's throne
Compared to waiting on a father's will?
To be the ruler of submissive kings
Is nought to one who makes his earthly aim
To satisfy his father's every want.
How can the sovereignty of all the worlds
Be weighed against the duty that a son
Owes to his father. Oh, my friend!
Where is that happiness you speak of.

ÂTREYA (*aside*). What a nuisance all this 'duty' is that he owes to his father! (*considering*) Well! never mind! I will put it in this way.

(*Aloud*) Oh! I didn't mean simply the enjoyment of the pleasures of *sovereignty;* there is something besides that for you.

JÎMÛT. Something besides? What mean you? Is not all
Exactly as it should be? In the path
Of virtue do my people walk—the good
Attain to happiness—my relatives
Are equal with myself: a regent holds
My place: the bounteous tree of Paradise
Gives to the poor man even past his wants.
Tell me what more remains? What may I do
Still further?

ÂTREYA. Well! You have an inveterate enemy in Matanga. While he is at large, however well governed your kingdom may be, it never can be safe in your absence.

JÎMÛT. What mean you? That Matanga means to seize
Upon my kingdom?

ÂTREYA. Certainly!

JÎMÛT. And pray why should he not? All I possess—
Even my very self, I do but hold
For others' benefit. My father's will
Stands in the way, or I had given up
All to Matanga. Why then offer me
Such worthless counsel? Let me rather do
All that my father ordered. Let us go
Hence to Malaya's mount, if we may find
Some hermitage in which to spend our days.
Thus he commanded me. So to the mount

We go.

ÂTREYA. So be it, as your Highness wishes.

(*As they walk on*)

O feel you not, my lord, the scented breeze
That blows from Malaya? How sweet! How cool!
Chasing away the trav'ller's weariness
Like the embrace of some fair loving spouse
Who welcomes his return. See how the spray
Borne on the wind, caught up from the cascade
That falls in broken foam upon the rocks
Scented with juice of fragrant sandal, thrills
Our inmost being!

JÎMÛT. Ah, my dearest friend!
This is indeed Malaya's hill. O what delight!
How sweet the fragrant odours from the groves!
For from the tree pierced by the elephants,
Thrusting their tusks in frenzy through the bark,
The scented juice pours forth; the caves resound,
Lashed by the ocean waves: the pearly rocks
Stained by the crimson dye that decks the feet
Of beauteous women passing to and fro.
Alas! Such sights recall my mind to earth
And earthly things. Come, let us choose some spot
Where we may dwell in peace!

ÂTREYA. As your highness wishes.

JÎMÛT. (*starting*). My right eye seems to throb! What may this mean?
I have no unfulfilled desire, nor wish

Ungratified, but what the sign portends
The wise have told us: can their words be false?
What think you means this omen?

ÂTREYA. It means that you are on the point of meeting some beloved object.

JÎMÛT. (*reflecting*). It must be so!

ÂTREYA. Sir! Look! Look! Surely this must be a grove in which ascetics dwell. Here are trees throwing a dense shade—the animals lying down peacefully without fear of being harmed—while the smoke ascends from the sacrifices laden with scent.

JÎMUT. Yes! You are right! This is a sacred grove!
Here are the trees—their bark stripped off to serve
As clothing! yet the strips are not too wide
In pity for the trees; and there the pots
Broken and old shine through the water's depth,
And worn-out girdles of the sacred grass—
Cast off—lie here and there—A Parrot chants
A verse of Sacred Scripture—learnt by heart
From hearing it repeated o'er and o'er.
Come, let us enter! (*They enter.*) O the tranquil charm!
This is indeed a hermit grove: the trees
Are tended by the daughters of the Saints,
From time to time the fuel freshly cut,
That feeds the fires burning in the shrines,
By their disciples, while the Saints delight
To teach the mysteries of sacred lore.

Even the trees, their heads bowed down by fruit,
Seem to pay homage to the coming guest,
And rain their flowers upon me, while the bees
Utter a hum of welcome. Ah ! this grove—
Peaceful and calm—shall be our dwelling-place.
Here find we rest from toil.

[*Sounds heard of music and singing.*

But what is this ?

ÂTREYA. Even the deer prick up their ears, and listen to the strain with their eyes closed, while from their mouths falls the half-chewed grass.

JÎMÛT. 'Tis even so !
The antelopes bend forward eagerly
To catch the sounds—a sweet melodious song
Joined with the plaintive lute, whose murmuring strings
Are as the hum of bees.

ÂTREYA. Who is this then singing in the sacred grove ?

JÎMÛT. Such is the sweetness of the heavenly strain
It must be that a goddess sings and plays !

ÂTREYA. Come then ! your highness ! let us enter !

JIMÛT. Yes !
My friend, you counsel well ! So let us go
Within and worship. Stay ! but let me think !
Perhaps we are not fit to cast our eyes
On such a holy sight : so let us hide
Behind this tree, and on the vision gaze,

Ourselves unseen.

[*They see* Malayavatî *and an* Attendant.

Malayavatî (*sings*)—

Goddess adored ! thy lovely form
Outshines the lily's radiant hue :
O grant me by thy mighty power
My heart's desire, for which I sue.

Jîmût. (*to* Âtreya). My dearest friend ! O what a lovely strain !
So clear ! so perfectly harmonious !

Attendant (*to* Malaya.). Your highness ! you must indeed be tired ! you have been playing and singing for a long while !

Malaya. How should I be tired ? You forget that I have been singing before the goddess Gaurî !

Attendant. And what is the use of your highness attempting to conciliate this implacable goddess ? You have been trying to gain her favour in every conceivable way : and all in vain.

Âtreya. Well ! after all it is only a girl. Why shouldn't we have a look at her ?

Jîmût. (*doubtfully*). Why not ? What is the harm ? After all there is no sin in looking at a damsel. But then if she caught sight of us, she might be alarmed and run away. So after all I think perhaps we had better stay where we are.

Âtreya. Very well, be it so ! (*after a moment*) Oh, your highness, what an entrancing sight ! Her beauty is as great as her skill ! Surely she must be a goddess, or a Nâgâ—or perhaps she is a Vidyâdhara or a Siddha princess.

JÎMÛT. My friend! Who she may be I know not

But this I know! If her abode be heav'n,
Then Hari's hundred eyes have all they need,
In gazing on her beauty. If she be
A Nâgâ—then the lowest depths of hell
Are lightened by her brilliancy, as though
The moon shone forth. If the Vidyâdharas
Claim her—then shall our family surpass
All others in renown. If she be born
Of Siddhas—then their glory shall prevail
Over the world.

ÂTREYA (*looking at* JÎMÛTAVÂHANA, *aside*). Here is a piece of good luck! At last he is fallen into the power of love—or rather, perhaps, I ought to say he has fallen into *my* power. However, he has been a long time about it!

ATTEND. Your highness! I say again, why play before this unrelenting goddess?

[*Throws down the lute.*

MALAYA. Don't show disrespect to the divine Gaurî! She has been very kind to me lately.

ATTEND. Very kind! In what form has she shown her favour, your highness?

MALAYA. She has indeed been very kind to me! To-day I was playing the lute. After a while I fell asleep, and the adorable Gaurî appeared to me in a dream, and said: My child! The sweet strains of your lute, and your devotion to me, please me exceedingly:

as a reward you shall gain a prince of the Vidyâdharas for your husband.

ATTEND. Why do you call this a dream? Surely the goddess has given you your heart's desire——

ÂTREYA (*overhearing all this*). Surely the time has come for us to make ourselves known to the princess! Let us go into the temple.

JÎMÛT. No! I will not!

ÂTREYA (*goes in and drags* JÎMÛTAVÂHANA *after him*) (*to the* Princess). Your highness! I salute you! What Chaturikâ says is perfectly true! Here is the husband promised by the goddess!

MALAYA. (*looking bashfully at* JÎMÛTAVÂHANA, *to her* Attendant). And, pray, who is this?

ATTEND. (*looking at* JÎMÛTAVÂHANA). From his exceeding beauty I think he must be the husband that the goddess promised you.

[MALAYAVATÎ *looks shyly at* JÎMÛTAVÂHANA.

JÎMÛT. (*to the* Princess)—

Lady! thy panting breast, thy drooping form—
Display thy weariness: O beauteous one.
Fear not! my presence shall not pain thee.

MALAYA. (*aside to* Attendant). Oh! I am filled with alarm! I cannot stand here face to face with him (*turns away*).

ATTEND. Princess! what means this behaviour?

MALAYA. I will not remain here in the presence of this man! Let us go elsewhere.

[*Makes as if to rise.*

ÂTREYA. Ah! she is really frightened! Shall I try and keep her for a moment, as long at any rate as I contrive to keep in my head anything I have had to learn?

JÎMÛT. Well! I don't know that there would be any harm in that!

ÂTREYA (*to* MALAYA.). May I ask your ladyship why you don't give the strangers a word of welcome?

ATTEND. (*looking at* JÎMÛTAVÂHANA *aside*). She looks pleased at his salutation. (*To* MALAYAVATÎ). Madam! The Brâhman speaks very reasonably. Guests should always be greeted respectfully. Why do you stand there lacking in decent civility to such a noble-looking person. Well! you may do as you like! I shall certainly go and speak to him. (*To* JÎMÛTAVÂHANA). Sir! Your Highness! I offer you my salutations! Will you honour me by taking a seat?

ÂTREYA (*to* JÎMÛT.). O my dear friend! she speaks admirably! Let us sit down and rest ourselves. (*They sit down.*)

MALAYA. (*to the* Attendant). May I ask you not to be so forward? Some one of the Ascetics of the grove might come by, and he would think me ill-behaved.

Enter an Ascetic.

ASCETIC. To-day obedient to his father's will
The Siddha prince, Mitrâvasu, has gone
In haste to seek Jîmûtavâhana—
The future King of the Vidyâdharas,

Who sojourns in this mount. The Siddha King
Would give his daughter, Malayavatî,
In marriage to Jîmûtavâhana.
She lingers, and the time may pass away
For midday sacrifice ere she return.
Therefore my lord and master Kauśika
Has bid me fetch her home without delay.
And I obedient to his word, I go
To search the Sacred Grove.

[*Looking round.*

Why ! what is this ?
Here is a footstep, and the mystic sign
Is clearly printed in the dust. (*Sees* JÎMÛT. *in front*).

Surely I see
A man of royal birth ! Upon his head
The kingly diadem : his arching brows,
Joined in their midst : his eyes like lotuses—
His chest broad as a lion's—and his feet
Signed with the sacred mark of sovereignty—
All show his majesty, and prove him lord
Of the Vidyâdharas. Away with doubt !—
This is indeed Jîmûtavâhana.
(*Seeing* MALAYAVATÎ).
And here the daughter of my lord—
(*Looking at both*). Kind fate !
I pray you look propitiously on both,
Who seem as if for one another made,
And grant them union.
(*Approaching* JÎMÛTAVÂHANA). Sir ! I salute you !
I bid your highness welcome !

JÎMÛT. (*preparing to rise*). Sir! I bow
Myself before you!

ASCETIC. Sit! I pray you sit!
"The guest is the superior of all."
Such are our master's words, You are the guest,
And therefore worthy of our reverence
Rise not, I beg of you, but let us give
To you our homage while you rest.

MALAYA. (*to the* Ascetic). Accept
My humble duty, Father!

ASCETIC. Ah! my child!
A worthy husband be your lot! But stay—
I have commands for you. The time is near
For offering up the midday sacrifice,
Therefore our Lord bids your attendance. Come!

MALAYA. Sir! I obey! Ah! I am torn in twain!
My spiritual Father bids me come,
My heart bids me remain: remain and gaze
Upon my future husband.

[*Goes out looking back at* JIMÛTAVÂHANA.

JÎMÛT. (*sighing and looking after* MALAYAVATÎ). She may go!
But still she leaves imprinted on my heart
Her beauteous image!

ÂTREYA. Well! You have seen all you wanted to see! You have heard all you wanted to hear! I suppose you are satisfied. As far as I am concerned, I am possessed with a raging hunger:

So let us go and see what these reverend fathers have got for us to eat.

JÎMÛT. Above our heads the lordly sun
Has reached the very summit of the heav'n,
And with his thousand rays burns up the earth.
See, like a fading tree, the elephant
Hardly endures the heat, and would assuage
His fever with the sandal juice: his ears,
Like fans, stir up the breeze around his face,
And with his trunk, he pours upon his breast
Water in plenteous streams. Let us depart.

[*Exeunt.*

END OF ACT I

ACT II

Enter one of the Princess MALAYAVATÎ'S Attendants.

ATTENDANT. The Princess Malayavatî has sent me to try and find her brother Mitrâvasu. He ought to have been here to-day, and she wants to know what has become of him. Here is someone coming in a great hurry! Why, it is Chaturikâ! (*Going up to* CHATURIKÂ). Hullo! where are you going in such a hurry? Do you want to cut me?

CHATURIKÂ. Oh! not at all—but her highness sent me to put this sandal-creeper arbour in order; she says she is burnt up with fever through the heat, and wants to go and sit there; so I am going back to tell her that it is ready.

ATTEND. Well, go and tell her! I hope it may do her good.

CHAT. Oh! I don't know much about that! I don't think it will do her 'fever,' as she calls it, much good: probably make it a good deal worse. That's my opinion. However, I must go and tell her that I have carried out her bidding.

Enter MALAYAVATÎ *with an* Attendant.

MALAYA. Oh! my heart! Thou madest me

dumb when I was in my lover's presence, and now thou art gone out to him of thine own accord! Alas! for thy selfishness. (*To* CHATURIKÂ). Show me the way to Gaurî's temple.

CHAT. Your highness! are you not going to the sandal bower?

MALAYA. (*confused*). Oh, yes! You have well reminded me! Come, let us go!

CHAT. (*aside*). What an absentminded state she is in! She can't get the goddesses' temple out of her head! (*To* MALAYA.). Madam! Here we are at the sandal bower! Perhaps it may do you good to go and sit in it.

MALAYA. (*entering, aside*)—

Lord of the darts whose tips are armed with flowers!
Thou work'st no ill on him whose beauty far
Surpasses thine: but thou art not ashamed
To strike at me, who am a helpless girl.

(*To* CHATURIKÂ). Tell me! why is it that this bower of sandal creeper, though its shades keep off the burning rays of the sun, does not allay my fever?

CHAT. Yes! Your highness! I know the cause of your fever; but I suppose you would not admit it.

MALAYA. (*aside*). Ah! she has found me out! (*Aloud*) Well! what is the cause? What is it that I would not admit?

CHAT. The cause is the man that you have in your heart.

MALAYA. (*going forward joyously*). The man? Where is he? Where is he?

CHAT. 'He!' what 'he' do you mean?

[MALAYAVATÎ *sits down and hangs her head in silence.*

CHAT. Well, I will tell you! The man in your heart is the one that was given you in a dream by the goddess, and whom you saw immediately after. He is as beautiful as Kâma, and he is the cause of your 'fever.' Believe me, the sandal arbour will not take it away.

MALAYA. (*aside*). Ah! she certainly has found me out! (*Aloud.*) Chaturikâ is a very good name for you, for you are so clever that it is impossible to hide anything from you; so I will tell you everything.

CHAT. You need not do that; I know everything already. You need not get into a state of 'fever,' for as sure as my name is Chaturikâ, you may depend on it that he who has once seen you will not know a moment's happiness without you. This is what I have found out.

MALAYA. (*in tears*). And what right have I to such happiness?

CHAT. Your highness! don't say that! Surely you know even Vishnu himself is not perfectly happy separated from Lakshmî.

MALAYA. Oh! You are very kind and flattering! But my fever rages the more because I recollect that I never spoke a word of welcome to him; and he will think me so awkward and ungainly. (*Weeps.*)

CHAT. Your highness! do not weep. (*Aside.*) But how can she help it? The fever of her heart afflicts her so that she cannot but weep.

(*Takes a plaintain leaf and fans her.*

MALAYA. (*stops her*). Oh! stop! Even the air from the plaintain leaf is hot.

CHAT. Madam! don't lay the blame on the plaintain leaf! It is the fever of your sight which makes the air from the plaintain leaf warm.

MALAYA. (*with tears*). O my dear Chaturikâ! it is all of no use! Nothing will give me any peace.

CHAT. Yes, there is something that would! Suppose '*he*' were to come here.

Enter JÎMÛTAVÂHANA *and* ÂTREYA.

JÎMÛT. O flower-armed god! Why am I still thine aim?
Have mercy on my heart already pierced
By arrows numberless. For as she gazed
On me, though for a moment, lo! her glance
Lit up the hermit grove, and made the trees
Shine out, all dappled with the rays of light,
Like skins of fleckéd antelopes.

ÂTREYA. My friend!
How has thy constancy departed!

JÎMÛT. What!
My constancy! are not my heart and mind
Beyond imagination calm and firm?

Have I not gazed upon the brilliant moon
Night after night? enjoyed the scented breath
Of lotuses? Has not the evening breeze
Been welcomed by me, loaded with perfume
Of jasmin flow'rs? Have I not heard the hum
Of bees that hover o'er the lotus beds?
O why reproach me in this hopeless state
With want of firmness? (*Reflects.*) Let me think again!
Is it not true? and my excuses false?
Else could I bear the darts against me aimed
By Kâma! You are right! How can I say—
My mind is firm and stedfast?

ÂTREYA (*aside*). This unfortunate reference of mine to his want of firmness has quite upset him. I must change the subject. (*To* JÎMÛT.) Sir! How is it that you have forgotten all about your parents and have come here?

JÎMÛT. And who should have a better right than thou
To ask the question? Therefore I will speak.
I had a dream, and in the dream I saw
Her whom I love, seated upon the slab
Of moonstone in this arbour: and her face,
All pale and wan, rested upon her hand.
She wept, and from her came reproaching words,
Because her love found no response in me.
Therefore this bower shall be my resting-place
To-day, the bower wherein I saw my love.

CHAT. (*listening anxiously*). Your highness! I hear footsteps! Some one is coming this way.

MALAYA. No one must find me here in this state of agitation! They might guess the cause. Let us hide behind the Asoka tree and see who it is.

ÂTREYA. Well! here is the sandal bower! Are you going in?

JÎMÛT. Even this sandal bower delights me not!
For she, whose presence made it radiant,
Has gone, and darkness reigns, as when the moon
Has left the face of night.

CHAT. Madam! You are in luck! Here is the very man you have set your heart upon.

MALAYA. (*with joy and alarm*). Yes! but I cannot stay here! I am so full of fear that I cannot remain anywhere near him. Perhaps he may see us.

CHAT. Your highness forgets! we are hidden!

ÂTREYA (*looking round*). Well, sir! Here is the moonstone seat.

(JÎMÛTAVÂHANA *sighs.*)

CHAT. Your highness! I hear some voices: let us listen, and hear what they say.

ÂTREYA (*touching* JÎMÛT.). Sir! don't you hear me? Here is the moonstone seat.

JÎMÛT. Ah! very true!
This is the moonstone seat, and on it sat
My lovely one, resting her pallid cheek
Upon her hand: with sighs her heaving breast
Was like to burst: and then her anger passed
When I delayed to soothe her, and she showed

Her love for me, with quivering lip! My friend! Let us recline upon the moonstone seat.

MALAY. (*reflecting*). Of whom is he talking? It seems as if it were someone with whom he has had a lover's quarrel.

CHAT. I don't know! let us listen and find out.

ÂTREYA (*aside*). My friend seems to like this kind of talk; I will try a little more of it. (*Aloud.*) Well! Sir! and what did you say to the beautiful damsel of your dream?

JÎMÛT. I said:

This moonstone seat, besprinkled with thy tears,
Is as if shedding dew, thy beauteous face
Mistaken for the rising moon.

MALAY. (*angrily*). Chaturikâ! what nonsense is this? Let us be off!

CHAT. (*seizing her hand*). Your highness! don't say that! It is *you* whom he saw in his dream: no one else would give him any pleasure.

MALAY. Well! I am not convinced! but I will stay and see what more he has to say about it.

JÎMÛT. Âtreya! Ah! a thought has crossed my mind,
I cannot see my love, so will I draw
Her lovely face upon this moonstone slab!
Go to the mountain side, fetch me some chalk!

ÂTREYA. Certainly, your highness! (*Returns.*) Sir! here is the chalk! You asked me for one colour, and I have brought you five!

JÎMÛT. My friend! I thank you.

[*Draws on the stone.*

The face of my beloved on the stone
Fills me with pleasure, while I gaze on her.
Her face in radiant glory, like the moon
Feasting the eyes.

ÂTREYA. Wonderful! How can you draw the likeness of one whom you cannot see?

JÎMÛT. Nothing to wonder at! Her lovely form
Is always in my mind! What wonder, then,
That I can draw her likeness?

MALAYA. (*in tears*). O Chaturikâ! It is quite clear what the end of the story is going to be. Let us go and see where Mitrâvasu is gone.

CHAT. (*aside*). Her impatience will surely lead to her own destruction. (*To* MALAYA.) Madam! Manoharâ has already gone to look for Prince Mitrâvasu; perhaps he may be even now on the way.

Enter MITRÂVASU.

MITRÂ. My father bids me find
The noble prince Jîmûtavâhana:
My father knows him for a virtuous prince—
A worthy son-in-law; for he has lived
Close by upon this mount. Therefore to him
He gives his daughter Malayavatî
In marriage. As for me, affection holds
Me bound to her so strongly that to think
I know not what. Jîmûtavâhana
Is a Vidyâhdara by birth, indeed
Clever and brave and wise.

Sought after by the good, of handsome form,
Modest withal. But on the other hand
His heart so full of pity, he would give
His life itself for any living thing.
Therefore I hesitate, my mind is full
Of doubt. When I behold the *noble prince*,
I give my sister up to him with joy.
But when I see the *man* all pitiful,
Then I repent! Jîmûtavâhana
Is in the sandal bower—so I am told.
Let me go in and speak with him.

[*Enters.*

ÂTREYA (*sees him; hastily*). Sir! Here is Mitrâvasu! Make haste! Cover up the picture you have been drawing. Perhaps he may see it.

[JÎMÛTAVÂHANA *places a plaintain leaf on it.*

MÎTRÂ. (*enters*). Sir! I salute you!

JÎMÛT. Mitrâvasu, I bid you welcome.

CHAT. Your highness! Prince Mitrâvasu has arrived!

MALAYA. Oh! what joyful news.

JÎMÛT. I trust that Viśvâvasu, the noble King of the Siddhas, is well?,

MÎTRÂ. He is well. I am here by my father's command.

JÎMÛT. What says his Majesty?

MALAYA. (*aside*). Now I shall hear what my father's orders are.

MITRÂ. King Viśvâvasu offers you his daughter Malayavatî in marriage. She is the life and soul of the family.

CHAT. (*smiling*). Well, your highness! are you still angry?

MALAY. (*smiling*). Have you forgotten? His heart is set on another.

JÎMÛT. (*aside to* ÂTREYA). My good friend! now we are in a difficulty.

ÂTREYA (*aside to* JÎMÛT.). Of course I know very well there is only one you care for. You had better dismiss the prince as politely as you can.

JÎMÛT. Sir! who would not desire the honour of being allied with the noble family of your highness? But, unfortunately, my heart is already engaged.

[MALAYA. *faints*.

ÂTREYA (*to* MITRÂVASU). What is the good of asking *him* whether he will or no? Go to his parents and ask *them*.

MITRÂ. (*aside*). This seems reasonable enough! Jîmûtavâhana will hardly refuse to listen to his parents. So I will go and put the matter before them, and get them to accept Malayavatî for him. (*Aloud to* JÎMÛT.). Well! So be it, your highness! We have made you our offer, and you have refused it.

MALAYA. (*coming to herself angrily*). What! Mitrâvasu still talking with him, after he has insulted us by his refusal?

[*Exit* MITRÂVASU.

MALAYA. (*aside with tears*).

What profit is my life, possessed by ill—
Filled with intolerable woe. This tree
Shall put an end to all my hopeless grief.

A creeper branch around my neck. [to Chaturikâ] Go! see –
See if Mitrâvasu has gone, for I
Would fain myself depart.

CHAT. (*aside*). What is the meaning of this? She has some hidden object in view. I will pretend to go, and hide myself where I can see what it all means.

MALAYA. (*taking the creeper branch into her hand*).
Mistress Divine! Thy promises are vain,
Nor hast thou giv'n thy child her heart's desire.
Grant me that happiness in other worlds
Denied to me in this.

CHAT. (*seeing it in terror*). Help! Help! Her highness is hanging herself.

JÎMÛT. (*coming forward hurriedly*). Where? Where is she?

CHAT. Under the Aśoka tree.

JÎMÛT Here is the very object of my love!

[*Takes* MALAYAVATÎ *by the hand and untwines the creeper.*

O lovely one! forbear! nor harm thyself!
Remove this creeper from thy hand, which vies
With it in beauty, barely strong enough
To pluck a flow'r. How should that hand perform
A deed so violent!

MALAYA. (*angrily*). Sir! who are you?
Let go, let go my hand! Do you presume
To stay my purpose? Must I be your slave
Even in death?

JÎMÛT. Why should I loose your hand

Caught in the guilty act! For you would place
The deadly noose round that fair neck of yours,
A neck that should be graced by strings of pearls.

ÂTREYA. What is the meaning of all this? Why should the princess try to hang herself?

CHAT. (*to* ÂTREYA). Cannot you see that your friend here is the cause of it?

JÎMÛT. I am the cause? I understand you not!

ÂTREYA (*to* CHAT.). What do you mean? Speak out plainly.

CHAT. Well, the truth is this. Your friend drew on the moonstone seat the picture of someone or other with whom he is in love, and then declined to accept the Princess, even when Mitrâvasu offered her to him. So in a fit of jealousy her highness determined to put an end to her life.

JÎMÛT. (*joyfully*). Ah! who is this? Is this indeed the child
Of Viśvavâsu, Malayavatî?
Except from ocean depths, how could there rise
A vision of such perfect loveliness,
From which the moon sprang forth. Ah, how my mind
Has cheated me!

ÂTREYA. I think you won't find any more fault with my friend now! Madam! your highness! If you don't believe me, go and look at the drawing on the moonstone seat!

[MALAYA. *bashfully tries to draw away her hand from* JÎMÛTAVÂHANA.

JÎMÛT. (*smiling*). No! I will not release you
till you see
My love depicted on the moonstone seat.

[*They enter the arbour.*

ÂTREYA (*taking the plaintain leaf off the moonstone seat*). See! your highness! here is the picture of the desire of his heart.

MALAYA. (*smiling*). Why! Chaturikâ. It looks exactly as if it were my likeness.

CHAT. 'Looks,' indeed! How can you say it 'looks' as if it were your likeness, when it *is* your likeness?

MALAYA. Well! he has made me feel ashamed of myself and my foolishness.

ÂTREYA. Now, sir! you may loose her hand, for your marriage according to the Gandharva rites has been completed. (*Looking off.*) Who is this coming in such a hurry?

[MESSENGER *enters.*

MESSENGER. Your highness! let me offer you my congratulations! You are accepted by the parents of Jîmûtavâhana as his bride.

ÂTREYA (*dancing with delight*). Now, my dear friend's desires are accomplished, as well as Malayavatî's; and something more than this, I shall very soon get what I want, and that is something to eat.

MESSENGER (*to* MALAYA.). The Crown Prince Mitrâvasu bids me to conduct your highness at once to the place for the performance of the marriage rites.

ÂTREYA. You low-born slave! and when you

have taken her away, how is my friend going to stay here alone ?

MESSENGER (*to* ÂTREYA). Cease your abuse ! (*To* MALAYA.) Madam ! the hour has come for the marriage. Follow me !

[MALAYAVATÎ *goes out with her* Attendants, *looking back affectionately at* JÎMÛTAVÂHANA.

HERALD (*behind the scenes*).

The dust in scented showers of crimson hue
Throws o'er the mount a splendour, like the haze
Of early dawn : while nymphs in joyful song
Announce to all the Siddha world the time
Of their princess' marriage : and the sound
Of tinkling anklets joyfully proclaims
The festal time. Your highness ! nought is left
To wish for ! All is granted ! All is yours !
The goddess has fulfilled her promise.

JÎMÛT (*joyfully*).

Why do we tarry ? Let us go within,
First to salute my father, then to take
Our part in joyous rites of festival.

[*Exeunt.*

END OF ACT II

ACT III

SCENE *the Flower Garden.*

Enter ŚEKHARAKA *drunk, with a cup in his hand, and his garment in confusion, followed by a* Slave *carrying a vessel full of wine on his shoulder.*

ŚEKHARAKA. There are only two gods I know anything about—one is Baladeva, and the other Kâmadeva. One is always drinking, and the other making love. (*Reels about.*) Ah! I am in luck, indeed! Here I am! I have my sweetheart with me, I am full of first-rate wine, and I have a garland on my head! What more could I want? (*Stumbles.*) Hullo! Someone is pushing up against me! Who is it? It isn't Navamâlikâ, is it?

SLAVE. No, sir! She hasn't come yet.

ŚEKHARAKA (*angrily*). Then why hasn't she, I should like to know. Malayavatî was married early this morning, so she has had plenty of time to come. (*Reflecting.*) Oh! I suppose the Vidyâdharas and the Siddhas are all drinking somewhere about in the garden along with their friends and relations in honour of this wedding. Perhaps Navamâlikâ is waiting for me there. So I will go and see if I can find her. What is Śekharaka without Navamâlikâ? [*Staggers about.*

Enter Âtreya *carrying a couple of female garments.*

Âtreya. Well, my dear friend has now gained his highest wishes. Probably he on his way here. (*The bees attack him.*) Hulloi what's the meaning of this? Why do thes villainous bees attack me? Oh! I see what it is! I have been dressed out and perfumed as the bridegroom's best man, and I have a garland of flowers on my head: what was intended as a mark of respect has simply become an annoyance. What shall I do? Perhaps I had better put on these crimson garments by way of a disguise which I have brought with me, and see what these rascally bees will do then. [*Puts on the garments.*

Śekharaka (*observing him*). Hullo! Well, here's Navamâlikâ! she has been long enough coming. I suppose she thinks I am angry, so she puts on her veil and turns away her head. Well, I will see if I can pacify her.

[*Goes up laughing, embraces* Âtreya, *and tries to put some betel in his mouth.*

Âtreya (*perceives the smell of wine, and turns his face away, holding his nose*). Pah! how disgusting! Well, I have escaped one nuisance only to fall in with another.

Enter Navamâlikâ.

Nava. The Queen has ordered me to tell the keeper of the garden to prepare the Tamala bower with especial care, for the bride and bridegroom are going there. So as I have carried out Her Majesty's command, I will now go and see if I can find my sweetheart Śekharaka. I haven't seen him for the last twelve hours, so he will be all the more pleased to see me. (*Sees him with* ÂTREYA.) Hullo! What's all this? He is making love to someone else. I will just wait here and see what it all means.

ŚEKHARAKA. Śekharaka is far too proud to bow down to Śiva, or Vishnu, or Brahma; but falls at the feet of Navamâlikâ.

[*Falls at his feet.*

ÂTREYA. You drunken scoundrel! Where do you think Navamâlikâ is?

NAVA. (*laughing*). Here is a joke! Śekharaka is too drunk to know the difference between me and Âtreya, and is making love to him. I will pretend to be angry, and make game of both.

SLAVE (*shaking* Śekharaka). This isn't Navamâlikâ! Here she is just coming up in a regular fury.

NAVA. Well, Śekharaka! and pray who are you making love to now?

ÂTREYA (*dropping the veil*). It is only I—and I am a Brâhman.

ŚEKHARA. (*recognizing* ÂTREYA). Hullo! you ape! you don't take me in. Catch hold of him, Slave, while I pacify Navamâlikâ.

SLAVE. As you command, sir!

ŚEKHARA. (*lets go* ÂTREYA, *and falls at the*

feet of Navamâlikâ). Navamâlikâ ! I pray you to forgive me !

Âtreya (*aside*). Now is the time to make off. (*Tries to escape. The* Slave *seizes him by his sacred cord, and it gets broken.*)

Slave. Ah ! you ape ! You would run away, would you ! (*Seizes him round the neck*).

Âtreya. O Navamâlikâ ! pray stand my friend and make him let me go.

Nava. (*laughing*). Yes ! if you will fall before me and touch the ground with your head !

Âtreya (*with anger*). A likely thing, indeed, that I, a Brâhman, and the friend of princes, should fall at the feet of a slave like you !

Nava. (*laughing*). Oh, never mind ! I will make you bow before I have done with you ! Now, my dear Śekharaka ! I am quite satisfied ; get up. (*Embraces him.*) But you see you have been insulting the bridegroom's greatest friend, and if Mitrâvasu, your master, hears of it, he will be very angry. You had better apologise at once.

Śekhara. Madam ! your word is law ! (*Embraces* Âtreya.) Sir ! pray excuse me ! it was only a joke : I thought you were one of my relations. (*Reels about.*) Where am I ? Who am I ? Am I Śekharaka, or am I not ? Am I a drunkard, or am I not ?

Âtreya (*hastily*). Certainly not ! You are perfectly sober !

Śekhara. Well, then, after all it is a joke. (*Takes off his upper garment and rolls it up, and offers it to* Âtreya *for a seat.*) Pray be seated, my new-found relation!

Âtreya. Heaven be praised! He is getting quieter! (*Sits down.*)

Śekhara. Now, Navamâlikâ! do you sit down on the other side of me, so that I can pay my respects to both of you at once!

[Nava. *sits down.*

Śekhara. Here, Slave, fill up this cup with wine. (*Takes the cup, and putting some flowers into the wine from the garland on his head, offers it kneeling to* Navamâlika.) Madam! I pray you take it, and pass it on.

Nava. Certainly! with pleasure! (*Takes the cup and gives it back.*)

Śekhara. (*offers the cup of wine to* Âtreya). This cup of wine has been sweetened by the touch of Navamâlikâ's lips. Let me offer it to you. It is the greatest honour I can pay you.

Âtreya. Śekharaka! you must excuse me! I am a Brâhman.

Śekhara. Well, then, if you are, where is your sacred cord?

Âtreya. Oh! that was torn off in the struggle with your servant.

Nava. Suppose you say some verses of the Veda, then!

Âtreya. No, I may not recite the Vedas so long as the scent of wine and perfume remains about. But I cannot argue with you. The Brâhman falls at your feet.

NAVA. (*stopping him hastily*). Oh, sir! you must not do that! Śekharaka, go away, go away! This really is a Brâhman. (*Falls down before* ÂTREYA.) Most Reverend Sir! do not be angry. This was only a joke!

ŚEKHARA. (*aside*). I think I had better make some sort of apology. (*Falls before* ÂTREYA.) Sir! Pray forgive me! I was under the influence of drink. Now I will be off with Navamâlikâ.

ÂTREYA. Pray don't distress yourselves! You have my free pardon.

[*Exeunt* ŚEKHARA., NAVA., *and* SLAVE.

ÂTREYA. Well! after all, the Brâhman has escaped an untimely end. But I am defiled by contact with the drunken fellow, so I must go and bathe. [*Exit.*

Enter JÎMÛTAVÂHANA *and* MALAYAVATÎ *dressed in wedding garments, with* Attendants.

JÎMÛT. (*looking intently at* MALAYAVATÎ)—

I look on her with loving glance: her eyes
Down to the ground she casts. I speak to her,
She answers not. She shrinks from my embrace
With trembling. She would fly me, and would go
With her old friends. My newly married bride—
Perverse—unreasoning, shy, becomes to me
More and more charming. (*To* MALAYA.) My beloved bride!

A vow of silence held me, wont to speak
In haughty tones. The fiery sun by day—
The moon by night—the raging forest fires
Scorched up my body: and my mind was turned
Away from all distractions. Such a vow
Was on me many days and nights—and now
At last, I reap the fruit of all my penance—
I behold thy face.

MALAYA. (*approaching*). How beautiful
His form! His words how flattering!

CHAT. Flattering! No! There is no flattery about it! It is all absolutely true.

JÎMÛT. Chaturikâ! lead the way to the flower garden.

(*Addressing* MALAYAVATÎ.) Come, my princess!
Thy fragile form, bowed down
With weariness, how should it bear the weight
Of these thy ornaments—the jewelled band
That circles round thy waist. Thy tender feet—
Scarce able to support thee—can they bear
Thy anklets? Ah! though unadorned, thy form
Is beautiful beyond comparison!
Why load thyself with wearying gold and gems!

[*They reach the flower garden.*

How sweet this pleasaunce! See the juice that falls
In scented showers from the sandal trees—
O how it cools the tessellated floor
That paves the arbour! See the peacocks dance

In wild excitement at the fountain's sound.
The water tawny with the dust of flow'rs
Flows through the trenches in abundant stream.
See how the bees keep joyous festival,
Their hum resounding through the creeper bower,
Their perfumed dust—the pollen of the flow'rs;
Meanwhile, the honey quaffed in copious draughts,
Shared with companions and friends—proclaims
A time of festival on every side.

ÂTREYA (*entering*). Sir! I salute you! Madam! I bid you welcome!

JÎMÛT. My dear friend! where have you been? You have been long in coming!

ÂTREYA. Sir! I have come as quickly as I could! but the truth is that I delayed a little on the road, for I wanted to see the Vidyâdharas and the Siddhas carrying out their festal customs in honour of your highnesses' wedding. Do come and look at them yourself.

JÎMÛT. Well, we will do as you wish! (*Goes forward.*)

See the Vidyâdharas: upon their heads
Crowns of Santâna flowers: on their limbs
The sandal ointment: while the sparkling gems,
That deck their garments, cast the rays of light
All round them! Underneath the spreading trees,

Joined with the Siddhas, see they drink the wine,
Just tasted by their wives.

ÂTREYA (*to* MALAYAVATÎ). Madam! your highness seems fatigued! Will you not rest upon this crystal seat?

JÎMÛT. My friend! You speak with thoughtful care!
The face of my beloved, once so cool
And fair as moonlight ray, now emulates
The lotus blossom reddening in the sun!
Let us sit down and rest.

MALAYA. I am content!
I will obey my husband's lightest wish!

JÎMÛT. (*raising up* MALAYAVATÎ'S *face and looking at it*)— My love!
Alas! how I have wearied thee in vain.
What need is there of flowers for thy face?
Of lovely hue—its eyebrows as the shoots
Of creepers, and thy budlike lower lip—
Is as the garden of Elysium.
All else is but a forest!

CHAT. (*to* ÂTREYA). You have heard how he paints her highness. Now let me paint you.

ÂTREYA. Chaturikâ! You must not make me conceited! There is only *one* person here who is worth looking at!

CHAT. Well! never mind! I should like to paint you!

ÂTREYA. Paint me, then! only do it so as to carry out your character for skill, and then, perhaps, I shan't be called an 'ape' again by Śekharaka.

CHAT. You looked just lovely this morning, when you stood with your eyes half shut! Stand like that for a moment, and let me paint you! [ÂTREYA *does as he is asked.*

[CHATURIKÂ *takes a tâmala shoot, squeezes it, and blackens his face.* JÎMÛTAVÂHANA *and* MALAYAVATÎ *look at* ÂTREYA *in amusement.*

JÎMÛT. Well! you are lucky to be painted like this with us for spectators.

(*Turns to* MALAYAVATÎ.)

My lovely one! thy smiling lower lip
Is as a *blossom*: but the *fruit* is seen
In these my eyes which gaze upon thee.

ÂTREYA (*to* CHAT.). What have you been doing?

CHAT. Have I not painted you?

ÂTREYA (*rubbing his face with his hand, and, seeing the black, raises his stick*). You daughter of a slave! What have you been about? And here in the presence of the Prince and Princess too! You have indeed made my face black! Well! it is of no good my staying here. I must be off. [*Exit.*

CHAT. Oh, dear! ÂTREYA is angry! I must go and pacify him.

MALAYA. You are not going, are you? What shall I do all alone?

CHAT. Alone, your highness! (*looking at*

JÎMÛTAVÂHANA *and smiling*). May you be alone for a long while. [*Exit.*

JÎMÛT. (*looking at* MALAYAVATÎ)—
The rosy flush that mantles o'er thy face,
As though it were a crimson lotus flow'r
Touched by the sun's fierce ray: thy pearly teeth
Like filaments, all white and radiant—
Why should the bee not sip his honey-dew
From such a face as thine?

Enter ATTENDANT *hurriedly.*

Sir! The noble Prince Mitrâvasu desires to see your highness on important business.

JÎMÛT. My dearest one! Mitrâvasu demands
My presence! Go within! I will rejoin
You presently.

Enter MITRÂVASU.

MITRÂ. (*aside*). The foe still lives! How shall I without shame—
Seeing I have not slain him—tell the Prince
Such evil news? 'The enemy has seized
Upon your kingdom!' Can I speak the words?
Yet I must tell him—then I will depart.

(*To* JÎMÛT.). Mitrâvasu salutes you! Noble Prince!

JÎMÛT. Welcome, Mitrâvasu! (*looking at him*). But how is this?
You seem cast down and vexed!

MITRÂ. And who should not,
With such a despicable foe in life
As vile Matanga?

JÎMÛT. Well! what has he done?

MITRÂ. He has attacked your kingdom: but the end
Must be his own destruction!

JÎMÛT. (*joyfully*). Were it true,
This would be joyous news!

MITRÂ. Therefore, my lord,
Send forth your orders! and the force arrayed
In martial panoply, their myriad hosts
Clouding the sun, with chariots that trace
Their course through highest heav'n, as though the sky
Were dark with storm, shall once again restore
Peace and prosperity to this your realm!
But yet, what need of armies? I alone,
Girt with my flashing sword, will smite the foe
Matanga, as a lion springs unseen
Upon a mighty elephant!

JÎMÛT. (*closing his ears*). Alas!
How cruel are his words! I will not heed
His angry threats! (*To* MITRÂVASU) Quite possible, my friend!
And even more than this with your strong arm
And your resistless might! But how should I—
I who would give unasked my very self
To save another—How should I consent
Even to keep my realm at such a price—
An act of fiendish cruelty? My friend!
There are no enemies but those within—
The vices which continually war
Against the soul! If you would please me, then,
Show pity to the miserable wretch

Who, covetous of pow'r, has sold himself
A slave to vice!

MITRÂ. (*angrily*). Pity, indeed! for one
So worthy of compassion—who has wrought
Such good to us.

JIMÛT. Alas! I cannot turn
His wrath aside! It must be so. (*To* MITRÂ.)
My friend!
Come in with me, I pray! hear my advice.
The day is over; see, the lordly sun,
Whose toil is all for others, who alone
Is to be worshippèd: who with his rays
Fills all the universe with light and life,
Waking the new-born lotus buds from sleep,
Nor stays his course through weariness!
Behold!
He goes to rest behind the Western Mount,
Meanwhile, the Siddhas loudly chant his praise.

[*Exeunt.*

END OF ACT III

ACT IV

Enter a Chamberlain *carrying a pair of crimson garments, followed by a* Messenger.

CHAMBERLAIN. I am supposed to be the ruler of the King's ladies; and I am always trying to catch them out tripping! Now here I am, become so old and feeble, that I am obliged to use a stick. So you see I am exactly like a King, for he bears a staff in the shape of a sceptre.

MESSENGER. And pray, where is your honour going?

CHAMBERLAIN. Well! The Queen has sent me to take some crimson garments as a present to Malayavatî and her son-in-law. The Princess is staying with her father-in-law, and I daresay you know Prince Jîmûtavâhana has gone to the sea-coast. Now the question is this, Am I to take these things to the Queen's daughter or to her son-in-law?

MESSENGER. I should think the simplest course will be to take the garments to Malayavatî. Probably the Prince has reached the sea-coast by this time.

CHAMBERLAIN. Well! Perhaps it would! But may I ask you, whither are you bound?

MESSENGER. I have been sent to remind

Mitrâvasu that a present must be given on the approaching festival of the New Year to the bride and bridegroom. So I am going to see what I can find suitable for the occasion.

[*Exeunt.*

The Seashore. Enter JÎMÛTAVÂHANA *and* MITRÂVASU.

JÎMÛT. My couch the fresh green grass: my seat a stone:
The branching trees my dwelling-place: my drink
The cooling water from the rill: my food
The roots: deer my companions. Such is life
Within the forest glade! But something lacks—
There is no need to ask, for all things give
Of their freewill: nor are there those who want
My help. Therefore my life is spent in vain.

MITRÂ. (*looking up*). The tide is flowing, Prince!

JÎMÛT. Yes! you are right!
I hear the sounds of monsters that emerge
From ocean wave, making the caves resound
With blows as they come forth all terrible.
The tide is rising, white with countless shells
Thrown up along the shore!

MITRÂ. O look! the sea
Comes in resplendent, as though set with gems,
The water scented with the shoots of clove
Chewed and spit out by monsters of the deep.
Let us ascend the cliff, before the tide
Come in and cut us off.

[*They ascend the cliff.*

JÎMÛT. Mitrâvasu,
Those heights are beautiful exceedingly,
Like snow-clad peaks covered with veil of cloud
White in the light of autumn!

MITRÂ. No! You see
No mountain peaks, but heaps of whitening bones.

JÎMÛT. Of bones! O wonderful! how came they there?
Why were these hapless creatures slain in heaps?

MITRÂ. They were not slain in heaps. These are the bones
Of Nâga victims: one by one they fell.
Day after day the ruthless King of birds
Came swooping down with wings that cleft the sea,
Their wind so violent: and as he rose
A Nâga was his prey.

JÎMÛT. Ah! wickedness!
Tell me! and then—

MITRÂ. The Nâga King, in fear
Lest all his people perish, prayed the King—
The ruthless King of birds—

JÎMÛT. What said he? Speak!
Was it to offer up himself, a sacrifice
To save his people?

MITRÂ. No! "Through fear of you,"
He said, as he addressed the winged King,
"The unborn offspring of my subjects die,
The young are carried off—and so our race
Will be destroyed: nor will you gain, your food

Will vanish off the earth. Therefore each day
A serpent shall be set apart for you, the food
For which you long. So may your highness
cease
To terrify my subjects."

JÎMÛT. (*with contempt*). Noble King!
Well hast thou guarded thy defenceless realm!
Was there not one of all thy thousand tongues
To say, "Take me! I offer up my life
To save my people"?

MITRÂ. So the Nâga king
Agreed to satisfy the king of birds.
Since then the Nâga bones, in whitening heaps,
Keep on increasing. Yes! and will increase!
For every day the ruthless King of birds
Seizes a helpless Nâga as his prey.

JÎMÛT. O horrible! And so will fools commit
Sins for their body's sake: a body worth
No more than dried-up grass: a body full
Of all impurity! Surely will fall
A judgment for the crime! Ah! could I give
My life to save—were it but only one
Of these unhappy serpents.

The Messenger *enters.*

MESSENGER. Well! I have reached the mountain peak at last: now I must try and find Prince Mitrâvasu. Oh! here he is with the bridegroom. (*Approaching.*) Your highnesses! I offer you my salutations.

MITRÂ. What is your errand?

[Messenger *whispers to* MITRÂ.

MITRÂ. Prince ! my father sends for me !

JÎMÛT. Farewell ! You must obey his orders.

MITRÂ. Jîmûtavâhana ! ere I depart,
Let me entreat you ! leave this loathsome place,
A place of evil omen ! [*Exit.*

JÎMÛT. I will go
Down to the sea, and walk along the shore.
[*Descends.*

Voice behind the scenes.

My son ! how can I bear to see thee slain
A sacrifice !

JÎMÛT. Ah ! what is that I hear—
A cry of agony ! a woman's voice !
What fears she ? I would know !

Enter ŚANKHACHÛDA, *a Nâga, followed by an old woman and a servant carrying a crimson robe.*

OLD WOMAN (*weeping*). Alas !
My son ! How can I bear to see thee slain
A sacrifice to-day ! Deprived of thee
Darkness will fall upon the Nâga world.

ŚANKH. Mother ! why weep ? why add to my distress
By tears ?

OLD WOMAN (*stroking his limbs*). Alas ! My son ! The King of birds,
All pitiless, will tear thy tender limbs.
[*Embraces him, weeping.*

ŚANKH. Mother ! enough of tears ! Fate leads us on,
Ev'n like a nurse, clasping the new-born babe

Close to her bosom from its very birth.
The mother is but second: for our lot
Is all decreed. How should you weep?

[*Makes as if going away.*

OLD WOMAN. My son!
Stay for one moment! Let me see thy face
Once more, I pray!

SERVANT. Prince Śankhachûda come!
Surely through grief thy mother has forgot
The king's decree! We may not stay!

ŚANKH. I come!

SERVANT (*aside*). Here is the fatal rock! Here he must stand
Wearing the badge of death!

JÎMÛT. (*sees them*). Ah! now I see
The woman and the son whose voices reached
My ear. Why does she weep? I see no cause
For all this grief and fear. Shall I approach
And ask them what it means? No! I will stay
And hear unseen their converse.

SERVANT (*making an obeisance*). Noble Prince!
The king's decree must be obeyed.

ŚANKH. Say on!

SERVANT. The Nâga king commands—

ŚANKH. My lord's commands
Shall be obeyed!

SERVANT. —"Upon the fatal rock
Clothed with this badge of death—the crimson robe—
Take up your place, and there await your fate.
You are Garuḍa's prey."

JÎMÛT. And does the king

Desert his subjects thus ?

SERVANT. Here is the robe !
Prince ! take it—put it on !

ŚANKH. (*respectfully*). Give it to me !

[*Puts it on.*

So I obey my lord !

OLD WOMAN (*seeing her son clothed in the robe*). My life is gone !
The thunderbolt has fallen !

[*Faints.*

ŚANKH. Mother ! revive !

SERVANT. The time is passing fast. The King of birds
Ere long will come to claim his destined prey.

[*Exit.*

OLD WOMAN (*coming to herself*)—
My child ! my son ! Son of a hundred vows !
When shall I see thee more ? Thy beauteous form
Doomed to destruction !

JÎMÛT. Ah ! how pitiless
The King of birds ! Indeed, of adamant
Must be his heart. Can he behold this child
Laid in his mother's lap, and turn away
Deaf to her tears and cries ?

ŚANKH. O mother ! cease
Thy lamentations ! There is none to heed !
All who would show compassion—all whose minds
Are more for others' good than for their own—
All who would mourn with us : all—all have gone

Into oblivion. Ah! none are left to show
Pity on us!

[*Wipes away his mother's tears.*

JÎMÛT. (*compassionately*). Unless I save from death
One who has been abandoned by his lord—
What virtue is there in me? I will go
And speak to them!

ŚANKH. Mother, be comforted!

OLD WOMAN. Comfort for me, indeed! Ah! there is none!
Thy king and guardian has cast thee off.
Who will protect thee?

JÎMÛT. (*coming forward*). Who? Why should not I?

OLD WOMAN (*mistaking him for* GARUḌA, *in terror*)—
O son of Vinatâ! The Nâga king
Has destined *me* for death! I am your food!

JÎMÛT. (*with tears*). Behold her love! Even the Nâgas' foe,
Seeing such grief and love—though pitiless—
Will show some pity!

ŚANKH. Mother! calm your fear!
He has no likeness to the King of birds.
Can you not see this man of gentle mien—
How has he aught in common with the son
Of Vinatâ, whose savage curving beak
Drips with the blood of Nâgas?

OLD WOMAN. Ah! my fear
Peoples the world with foes!

JÎMÛT. Mother! fear not!

I, a Vidyâdhara, have come to guard
Thy much-loved son!

OLD WOMAN (*to* JÎMÛT.). My son! what welcome words!
I pray you, say them once again!

JÎMÛT. What need
Of promises? My deeds shall prove their truth!
Give me the robe, that I may put it on,
Marking myself for death; so will I give
My body as an off'ring to the son
Of Vinatâ, and save your child!

OLD WOMAN. Ah! no,
Such must not be! Surely thou art a son
To me as Śankhachûda; even more—
For thou hast freely given thyself—thy life—
To save my son, deserted by his kin.

ŚANKH. O noble man! how different his mind
From that of worldly men! He casts away
His life, as though it were but straw, to save
Another's life. And yet in times gone by
The wise Viśvâmitra all humbly took
Dog's flesh at a Chandâla's hand, to save
Himself from starving. Gautama, the sage,
Slew Nâdijangha, though to him he owed
A kindness: and Garuḍa daily feasts
Upon the Nâgas. Even so the wise—
The great—the good—value their own lives most.
(*To* JÎMÛT.) But thou—far in advance of these—hast shown
Pity unasked for me, for thou hast giv'n
Thy life for mine. I pray! Do not insist!

Bethink you! beings of no account are born—
And live their lives, and die, and leave no trace
Behind—and such am I: but virtuous men
Who think not of themselves, but sacrifice
Their lives for others—such indeed art thou—
How come they into being! Be content!
Do not insist on death! Cease thy resolve!

JÎMÛT. O Śankhachûda! put no obstacle
To my desire's fulfilment! Now at last
Have I attained my wish: for I have gained
The long-sought opportunity for good
That I have prayed for: so no argument
Shall change my will! Give me the crimson robe—
The badge of death.

ŚANKH. I pray you, force me not!
I cannot yield! O how should I defile
My family of pure, unsullied fame
By such a deed? Devise some other plan,
If we are worthy of your love, to save
My mother's life!

JÎMÛT. A plan! Devise a plan!
What plan but this! Your mother lives with you,
And dies with you. My life shall ransom yours
From death! Give me the crimson robe you bear,
And I will mount the rock of sacrifice.
Do you depart at once, and leave this home
Of death, and let your mother be your charge
Beyond all other things, nor let her look
Upon the rock of slaughter, lest she die

O'erwhelmed with pity.
See you not the bones
Of countless perished Nâgas in this place
Where awful darkness broods ? While flapping wings
Of vultures hide the sun, and hover o'er,
Eyeing with greediness the flesh that falls
Out of their beaks that drip with blood ; and rows
Of jackals howl unceasing, at the smell
Of reeking flesh, that lies in seas of blood.

ŚANKH. How should I not ? The serpents' burial place—
The place which charms Garuḍa—where he finds
His daily serpent meal—before me lies—
As terrible as that fell god who wears
Around his neck for ornament the skulls
And bones white as the moonlight.

JÎMÛT. Hold ! Enough !
What mean these terror-striking images ?
They move me not ! My mind is firmly fixed !

ŚANKH. The time is close at hand, Garuḍa comes !
Mother, depart ! May I be born again ;
Whatever be my state, O may'st thou be
My mother still !

OLD WOMAN. Are these thy parting words,
My dearest son ? I cannot leave thee thus—
But I will die with thee !

ŚANKH. Ere I obey
My lord's commands, I go on pilgrimage.

There is a sacred place close by : full soon
Will I return.

[*Exeunt* Śankhachûda, *carrying the crimson robe with him.*

Jîmût. Fortune is mine, my wish
Is gained at last !

Enter Chamberlain *carrying some red garments.*

Chamberlain. Your highness ! pray accept
My salutations ! See, the Queen has sent
These garments as a present.

Jîmût. (*aside*). Give them me !
My union with Malayavatî
Has borne good fruit indeed. (*To* Cham.)
Salute the Queen
From me. Farewell. [*Exit* Chamberlain.
(*Putting on the red garments*)—
This is indeed a gift
In season ; and it fills me with delight.
For I can give myself, arrayed in these,
A ransom for another. Lo ! the wind
Rises in violence ! It shakes the mass
Of Mount Malaya. See ! Garuḍa comes !
The sky is darkened by his mighty wings,
As though the clouds that usher in the end
Were spread abroad. The elephants that bear
The quarters of the earth tremble and quake.
His radiant form lights up the universe,
As with the glory of a dozen suns.
I will await him on the fatal rock
In Śankhachûda's place. [*Mounts the stone.*

My body thrills
With rapture as I mount the rock. The touch
Of Malayavatî, perfumed with juice
Of sandal, does not give me one tenth part
Of all the joy I feel, when I embrace
The rock of sacrifice. Why should I speak
Of her, my bride? Even a child, who sleeps
Upon his mother's lap in careless ease,
Feels nought of my contentment, as I lie
Upon the rock.

Enter GARUḌA.

GARUḌA. I come to seize my prey,
My flight through space all swift and terrible.
I flew along—I saw the full round moon—
And thought of Śesha, curling up himself
Into a circle, through his fear of me.
I met the Dawn, the eldest of our race,
He greeted me with joy: and as I passed
The steeds which drew the chariot of the Sun
Started aside in terror. On I flew,
My wings, vast as they are, more widely still
Stretch out extended; from their farthest ends
Hang down, as though in dusky wreath, the
clouds.

JÎMÛT. (*to himself*)—
From this, the sacrifice I gladly make,
More and more merit may I still obtain,
And win in after births, for others' good,
A body to be sacrificed again.

GARUḌA (*sees* JÎMÛTAVÂHANA)—
Now I am come, and here upon the rock

I see the Nâga victim, offered up
To save his fellows ; in the crimson robe
He lies, as if his heart, broken through fear
Of me, had dyed his garments red with blood.
I will swoop down, and with my curving beak,
Fiercer than any thunderbolt, will tear
His breast in twain !

[*Flowers rain down and drums are heard*

O wonderful ! Why falls
This rain of fragrant flowers, at which the bees
Rejoice ? Why do the echoing drums resound
Along the sky ? (*Smiling.*) The tree of Paradise
Surely is shaken by the furious wind.
My wings stir up, and casts her flowers down
To earth : the clouds give forth their sullen roar,
To herald in destruction to the world !

JÎMÛT. O happy that I am ! I have attained
My heart's desire !

GARUḌA (*seizes* JÎMÛTAVÂHANA). But how is this ? He seems
Unlike a Nâga ! Still he will assuage
My greed for serpents' flesh. So I will bear
Him off to Mount Malaya's topmost peak,
And there my hunger he shall satiate.

[*Exeunt.*

END OF ACT IV

ACT V

Enter Messenger.

MESSENGER. "For one beloved, affection makes us dread
Evil and death, though he be safe at home.
How much more should we fear when far away
In some lone place, he dwells apart from men."

And this is the case with King Viśvâvasu. For his son-in-law, Jîmûtavâhana, has gone away to a region terrible through the neighbourhood of Garuḍa, the King of the Birds. Nothing has been heard of him since he left. So I am going to try and find the prince. Well! Here I see King Jîmûtaketu in the distance, with his Queen and the Princess Malayavatî.

Behold the royal sage! with linen robes
Whose folds are like the ripple on the sea,
White as the foam! and by him sits his Queen
Adorning him as Ocean is adorned
By sacred Ganges—both of excellence
And fruitfulness unrivalled: at their feet
Sits Malayavatî, the fair Princess.

Scene I

Enter King Jîmûtaketu, *his* Queen, *and* Princess Malayavatî.

The King. Mine has been all the joys of youth: my realm
All glorious: devotion ever filled
My mind: Jîmûtavâhana has gained
The praise of all: his wife is by our side,
As noble as himself. All has been mine!
Is it not time to meditate on death—

Messenger (*coming in suddenly*)—of Prince Jîmûtavâhana.

King. Avaunt!
Ah! what ill-omened words.

Queen. The gods avert
The omen!

Malaya. Ah! my heart within me sinks!

King. What is your news? What of his highness? Speak!

Messenger. Your Majesty! The King Viśvâvasu
Has bid me ask you, for he fain would know,
How fares the Prince? What answer may I take
Back to my lord?

King. How? What say you? My son—
Is he not with the king?

Queen. Why this delay?
Where can my son be gone?

King. It is for us,
No doubt, that he is gone away! His thoughts

Are ever set on us.

MALAYA. May it be so!
Indeed! *I* fear the worst!

MESSENGER. Your Majesty!
Command me! Say what answer I may give.

KING. I know not what to say! My mind is filled
With dread! "Jîmûtavâhana delays!"
That is your answer! Ah! my son! my son!
(*Looking at the sun*) Life-giving orb! O may thy thousand rays!
O eye the guardian of three worlds! make clear
The glory of my son.

[*A crest jewel falls at their feet.*

Oh! what is this?
As though the wind had torn a crimson star
From highest heav'n, and cast it down to earth!
O see! Its rays are like a mass of blood,
Mine eyes are dazzled by its brilliant light.
(*All look at it.*)
It is the jewel from a crest, with flesh
All raw and bloody hanging to it!

QUEEN (*mournfully*)— Ah!
It is my son's! Alas! he has been seized
A victim by Garuḍa!

MALAYA. (*aside*). God forbid!

MESSENGER. Most mighty king! let me allay thy fears!
Here many jewels, torn from Nâga crests,
Lie on the ground.

KING (*to the* QUEEN). Reason may be perchance

In what he says!

QUEEN. My son may even now
Have reached the palace of Viśvâvasu.
(*To the* Messenger)—
Go and find out at once if this be so.

[Messenger *exit*

KING. O may it prove to be a Nâga's crest!

Enter ŚANKHACHÛḌA *wearing red garments.*

ŚANKH. My pilgrimage is o'er, and I return
Whence I set out. Here is the slaughter rock,
The deadly stone; but the Vidyâdhara,
Where is he gone? Alas! he has been borne
On high, seized by Garuḍa's talons—torn
In pieces. (*Weeps.*) Ah! my dearest, truest friend,
Thou filled with pity, though there was no need—
More than a friend—gavest thyself for me!
Where art thou gone? Ah! wicked that I am!
My crime is past forgiveness! I have lost
All chance of merit by self-sacrifice
For all my kin: and I have disobeyed
My sovereign lord! O wretched that I am!
Saved by another: I have been deceived—
Nor will I live to be the mark of scorn,
But following the tracks of blood that lie
In streams upon the sacrificial stone,
But getting less and less, as in their course,
The ground—the trees—are sprinkled with the drops.

QUEEN (*anxiously*). Your Majesty! Pray, who is this? His words

Of grief trouble my heart!
ŚANKH. Ah! jewel crest!
A jewel, such as all three worlds combined
Could ne'er bring forth! When shall I see thy like?
Alas! My sight is well-nigh gone!
KING. Take heart.
This jewel crest is his! Some bird has torn
It, taking it for flesh, from off his head,
Dropping it on the ground.

QUEEN (*embracing* MALAYAVATÎ). My child! be calm!
Beauty like thine, was never meant to bear
The pangs of widowhood!
MALAYA. May it be so!
KING (*to* ŚANKH.). Pray tell me, sir! how did you lose
Your jewel crest?
ŚANKH. Alas! it was not mine!
KING. Whose is it, then?
ŚANKH. My voice all choked with grief.
Forbids my utterance!
KING. This grief of thine
Seems overwhelming! Tell it me; it may
Be less unbearable!
ŚANKH. Then I will speak:
I am a Nâga: by my king's command
I was appointed for Garuḍa's food.
But why delay? for even while I speak
The tracks of blood grow faint—impossible
To follow up: but in one word: my life
Was saved by a Vidyâdhara, who, filled

With pity, gave himself to death for me.

KING. And who except Jîmûtavâhana
Could e'er have offered up himself? My son—
This noble deed. Know when you tell the tale,
You say the name, "Jîmûtavâhana."

QUEEN. Alas! my son!

MALAYA. The evil I foresaw
Has come to pass.

SANKH. (*with tears*). Oh! woe is me! my crime
Has brought this evil on them! Surely these
Must be my saviour's parents! What could come
Save poison from a serpent's deadly mouth?
Ah! Śankhachûda! how hast thou repaid
Thy generous friend, who sacrificed himself
For thee! How shall I kill myself? But first
My aim must be to comfort them.

QUEEN (*to* MALAYA.). My child!
Without Jîmûtavâhana how can we pass
Our life on earth?

MALAYA. Belovéd! Shall I see
Thy face no more?

KING. My son! my noble son!
Even in death thy duty as a son
Was not forgotten, casting at my feet
Thy jewelled crest! (*Takes it up.*) And is this all I have
Left of my son? Alas! this sparkling gem
Against my feet continually pressed
In awe and reverence, polished by their touch,
As by a touchstone: never working ill
To any living creature: ah! that gem

Pierces my heart!

QUEEN. Jîmûtavâhana!
To thee the highest earthly pleasure seemed
Obedience to thy father's will: and now
My dearest son, the truest happiness
Is thine in Paradise.

KING. My loving spouse!
How can we live without him? These are words
Of cruel comfort!

MALAY. Father! give to me
The jewel crest, the outward mark he wore
Of rank, and let me wear it next my heart.
Adorned with this, upon the funeral pile,
I will efface the pain that burns me up.

KING. And what but that is left for all of us?
My wife! why are you troubled?

QUEEN. Mighty King!
Why do we then delay?

KING. There is no need!
The sacrifice is burning on the hearth,
The purifying flame: with that light up
The pile, and in the fires our life shall end!

ŚANKH. O wretched that I am! I have destroyed
A noble family! What shall I do?
(*To the* KING) It is not meet that such a deed as this
Should be performed without due thought. For fate
Makes sport of men! Perchance the King of Birds
Will let your son go free, finding his prey

Is not a Nâga! Therefore let me trace
Garuḍa's course, marked out in lines of blood.

QUEEN. May the gods grant me to behold my son
Once more!

MALAYA. Would it were possible! Could I
Believe that this thy prayer were heard.

KING (*to* ŚANKH.) My son!
O may thy words prove true! But as for us!
We cannot go without the sacred fire,
A fellow-traveller along the road.
Do thou pursue Garuḍa's track, and we
Will fetch the fire that burns upon the hearth,
And follow thee. [*Exeunt.*

ŚANKH. Now will I find the foe.
[*Walks about looking.*
Ah! there I see him, on the topmost height
Of Mount Malaya; with his gory beak
He ploughs its sides: his blazing eyes, like flame,
Scorch up the forest trees. The earth is torn
And furrowed by his adamantine claws.
[*Exit.*

END OF SCENE I

SCENE II

GARUḌA *seated on a rock, and* JÎMÛTAVÂHANA *lying before him.*

GARUḌA. A wonder such as this I never saw
At all my Nâga feasts, since I was born.
He shows no pain or terror, even joy—

I know not why! He is not faint: the blood
Is draining from him, yet he has not lost
His constancy. O see! his limbs are torn,
But yet his face shows peace and happiness.
Signs of delight are on him, and his glance
Is of affection. I would know what means
This strange behaviour: therefore I will cease
To tear him, and will ask him whence he comes,
And who he is.

[*Goes in front of* JÎMÛTAVÂHANA.

JÎMÛT. My blood is pouring forth,
Yet flesh remain, nor do I see in you
Satiety: why, then, cease eating?

GARUḌA (*aside*). Ah!
How wonderful! His voice is loud: he shows
No weakness. (*To* JÎMÛTAVÂHANA.) From thy heart my savage beak
Has drunk thy blood: thy constancy has gained
My heart: tell me thy name?

JÎMÛT. No! while the pangs
Of hunger still remain, I will not speak—
Take of my flesh and blood and satisfy
Thy craving!

Enter ŚANKHACHÛDA *hurriedly.*

ŚANKH. O Garuḍa! cease to act
So recklessly! I pray thee let him go!
He is no Nâga! See! the king has sent
Me for thy meal!

[*Bares his breast.*

JÎMÛT. Alas! my hopes are gone,
His coming has deprived me of their fruit.

GARUḌA. But how is this? Both of you bear the mark
Of sacrifice: which is the Nâga? Speak!

ŚANKH. How canst thou doubt? Is not the mystic sign
Upon my breast? Upon my limbs the scales
That show the serpent? Seest thou not my tongues
Of double form? my head with triple hood,
Through which my sighs resound, with whistling wind—
Sighs wrung from me by grief unbearable?
And seest thou not the gems which deck my hoods,
Distorted by the mass of smoke and fire
That rises from my poison?

GARUḌA (*looking at each alternately*).
Who is this?
I pray thee tell me! Whom have I destroyed?

ŚANKH. This is Jîmûtavâhana, the Prince
Of the Vidyâdharas! In ignorance
Thou hast destroyed him, cruel as thou art.

GARUḌA. Alas! is this Jîmûtavâhana,
The Prince of the Vidyâdharas, whose fame
Is sung by bards and minstrels, as they roam
From clime to clime. Ah! often have I heard
His glory hymned—in earth's remotest bounds—
In peaceful valleys—on the mountain peaks—
In hill-side caverns—even on these heights—
Where is his name unheard? Ah! I have sunk
Head first into the pit of sin.

JÎMÛT. My lord!

Why art thou troubled ?

ŚANKH. Is it not indeed
The time for trouble ? Thou should'st hurl me down
To lowest hell : for coward that I am,
My body has been saved from death by thee
Giving thine own.

GERUḌA. Alas ! this noble Prince !
His body willingly became my prey,
And saved a Nâga's life, whose time had come
To satiate my greed ! How horrible !
Ah ! What a sin is mine ! For I have slain
One who has all but reached the perfect state
Of righteousness. What is there left for me ?
How expiate my crime ? Except the flame
Should burn me up, and purge my sin away.
The fire ! Where shall I find it ? (*Looking round.*) Ah ! I see
Some persons near, and in their hands the fire !
I will await them.

ŚANKH. Prince ! Your parents come !

JÎMÛT. O Sankhachûda ! sit by me and cast
Thy garment o'er me ; hide my bleeding limbs ;
For if my parents saw my body torn
And mangled by Garuḍa, they would die !

[ŚANKHACHÛDA *spreads the garment over* JÎMÛTAVÂHANA.

Enter KING JÎMUTAKETU, *the* QUEEN, *and* MALAYAVATÎ *bearing the sacred fire.*

KING. My dearest son ! Jîmûtavâhana !
When you, with pity filled, gave up your life

To save the Nâga, why did you not stop
And think within yourself: My death will save
But one! I die, and with me, parents—wife—
My family—all die with me.

QUEEN (*to* MALAYA.). My child!
Weep not! or you will quench the sacred flame!

GARUḌA. Ah! who is this who says: "My dearest son!
Jîmûtavâhana!" Who can it be,
If not his father? So the fire he bears
Shall carry out my wish! But in his face
I dare not look for shame? Why should I stay
To ask for fire? Is not the ocean near,
With fire beneath it? Kindled by my wings
Into a fiercer flame, with flickering tongues
Waving with pleasure, like the tongues of death,
By which the world itself shall be consumed—
The sea licked up in mouthfuls, as they glide
Over its surface—into this I cast
Myself.

JÎMÛT. That will be all in vain! Your sin
May not be expiated thus!

GARUḌA (*making an obeisance*). Then speak!
Most noble one! and say what shall I do
To gain forgiveness?

JÎMÛT. See! my parents come!
I must salute them first!

GARUḌA. I wait your will!

KING (*joyfully*). Ah! fortune favours us! Our dearest son
Awaits us here—he lives—the King of Birds
Stands as a suppliant before his feet!

QUEEN. My prayer is heard! and I shall see his face,
His form uninjured!

MALAYA. Ah! I see my lord!
I scarce believe it!

KING (*approaching* JÎMÛTAVÂHANA)—
Come to my embrace!
Come to thy father!

[JÎMÛTAVÂHANA *attempts to rise: the garments fall off, and he faints.*

ŚANKH. Prince! revive! revive!

KING. And art thou gone—gone without look or sign!

QUEEN. My son, wilt thou not speak a word to me?

MALAYA. My husband! Are thy loving parents, then,
Not worth a glance?

ŚANKH. Ah! wretched that I am!
My life has been preserved, another dies
For me! Would I had died unborn! for grief,
Surpassing death, consumes my heart,
Moment by moment!

GARUḌA. Ah! This evil comes
From me! All base and wicked as I am!
What can I do!

[*Fans* JÎMÛTAVÂHANA *with his wings.*

Revive! Revive!

JÎMÛT. [*to* ŚANKHACHUDA]. My friend!
Comfort my parents!

ŚANKH. Let me minister

To thee, most noble King—Madam, to thee,
Such comfort as I can. Your son revives!
Do you not see he lives? And for your sake
Alone, he lives.

QUEEN. My son, thou art the prey
Of cruel death, even before our eyes!

KING. Ill-omened words! Do you not see he lives?
Console his weeping bride!

QUEEN (*weeping and covering her face*)—
Ill-omened words
Begone! I will not weep! Be comforted,
My dearest daughter, Malayavatî,
Look on your husband!

MALAYA. Ah! it is indeed
My husband's face!

KING. When I behold my son,
Whose strength is gone, whose life is ebbing fast,
How should my heart, insensible, not break
Into a thousand pieces!

MALAYA. Ah! my mind
Is evil, or I should cast off my life,
For sympathy with him, whose end is near.

QUEEN (*to* GARUḌA). How could'st thou wreck this body of my son?
All fresh and beautiful in fairest youth.
Hadst thou no care?

JÎMÛT. What evil has he done?
Is not my body just the same? a hideous thing,
Full of all evil, but a mass of flesh,

And blood, and bones, o'er which the skin extends
Its covering.

GARUḌA. O noble-minded man!
Ah! see my pain! The flames of deepest hell
Already scorch my being! Tell me how
I may be purified from this my sin.

JÎMÛT. Yes! I will tell thee, if my father give
Me leave.

KING. Speak on, my son!

JÎMÛT. Garuḍa, hear!

GARUḌA (*making an obeisance*)—
I am thy slave!

JÎMÛT. Cease from destroying life;
Repent thee of thy former evil deeds;
Lay up a store of merit; do good works;
By kindly love remove this fear of thee
That dwells in living creatures: so thy sin—
The sin which thou hast wrought—destroying life,
May cease to bring forth fruit, but, in the sea
Of merit plunged, may all be swallowed up,
Even as a grain of salt in Ocean depths.

GARUḌA. So will I do! for lying in the depths
Of ignorance, I have been roused by thee.
Henceforth I will no more destroy the race
Of living creatures. Let the Nâgas play
Over the ocean, in their multitudes,
In peace and happiness: and in the groves
Of sandal, let their damsels sing thy praise.
The morning sun may tinge their glowing cheeks

With crimson hue; their loosened hair may fall
All flowing to their feet, black as the cloud
Of evening: they may faint with weariness:
But still their saviour's praise unceasingly
Shall rise.

JÎMÛT. I am content! Be firm! Change not!
(*To* ŚANKHACHÛDA.) Depart! go to thy home!

[ŚANKHACHÛDA *hesitates, and stands with head hanging down.*

Why tarriest thou?
Thy loving mother waits in anxious dread
To learn thy fate; perchance thou hast been torn
In pieces by Garuḍa!

QUEEN. Blest indeed
The mother who beholds the son she loves,
With form uninjured, though the King of Birds
Had all but seized him!

ŚANKH. What thou sayest is true!
O could the Prince be saved!

JÎMÛT. Ah! now I feel
The agony that racks my limbs: delight
In doing good obscured the sense of pain,
But o'er me now, the darkness closes in.

[*Sinks dying.*

KING. My son! why dost thou fall?

QUEEN. Alas! my son!
His life is gone!

MALAYA. My husband! best beloved!
Why dost thou leave us?

JÎMÛT. (*trying to put his hands together*)—
Śankhachûda ! place
My hands together !

ŚANKH. (*placing* JÎMÛTAVÂHANA'S *hands together*). Ah ! the world has lost
Its lord.

JÎMÛT. (*looking at his father and mother with eyes half closed*)—
O Father ! Mother ! hear my words !
The last that I shall speak ! My eyes are dim ;
My limbs are failing me : I cannot hear
Your voice : alas ! my breath is going fast.
From this the sacrifice I gladly make,
More and more merit may I still obtain,
And win in after births, for other's good,
A body to be sacrificed again.

[JÎMÛTAVÂHANA *dies.*

QUEEN. Ah ! he is gone ! O my devoted son.
Devoted to thy parents ! joy of earth !
Where art thou gone ? O when shall I behold
My son again ?

KING. Jîmûtavâhana,
Joy of the nations ! Ah ! where art thou gone !
Canst thou not answer me ? Bereft of thee,
In whom all virtue dwelt—love, patience, truth,
The world is empty ! Whither shall we go
For pity, now the pitiful is gone !

MALAYA. Alas, my husband ! how canst thou forsake
Thy loving wife ? Ah ! Cruel that I am !
Why do I live ?

Śankh. O Prince! where art thou gone?
Forsaking those who love thee more than life!
Ah! I will follow thee!

Garuḍa. What can I do?

Queen (*looking up with tears*). Ye gods, our guardians! come, I pray, and bring
The heavenly nectar! O with that restore
My son to life again!

Garuḍa (*aside*). I may atone
For that my crime: so will I pray the gods,
And they shall send the heav'nly shower down,
And bring Jîmûtavâhana again
To life. Nor only so! but all the bones
Of Nâgas, who in times gone by were slain
By me. But if they will not hear my prayer,
My wings with furious blast shall turn to foam
The waters of the Ocean: at my eye
The Sun shall scorch and fall from heaven: my beak
Shall dash Kuvera's club in pieces: break
The thunderbolt of Indra: rend the net
Borne by the lord of Waters: in the fight
I will subdue the gods and rain from heav'n
To earth the show'r of immortality.

[*Exit.*

King (*to* Śankhachûda). O why dost thou delay? Collect the wood!
O let us build the funeral pile, and die
With our beloved son!

Queen. Make haste! Make haste.
Come, let us join him! Oh! he is in pain,
Bereft of us.

ŚANKH. The pile is all prepared!
Shall I not go before you, on the road
To meet your son!

KING (*looking at* JÎMÛTAVÂHANA). Then let us mount the pyre!
O head that wore the diadem! O eyes
Like lotuses: O form divine: O hand
Marked with the Mystic Sign: how hast thou gone!
Is it for my misdeeds that thou hast lost
The sovereignty of the Vidyâdharas?

MALAYA. Gaurî divine! Where is the noble Prince,
Of the Vidyâdharas, my future spouse?
Thy promises have failed! My hopes are gone.

Enter GAURÎ.

GAURÎ. O mighty king! act not so hastily!
Forbear!

KING. Ah! Gaurî! Blessèd be the sight!

GAURÎ (*to* MALAYA.). My child! how could I ever *seem* to speak
Words that are false? (*To* JÎMÛTAVÂHANA) With thee, my noble son,
I am well pleased, for thou hast offered up
Thy life to save the Nâga world!

[*Sprinkles* JÎMÛTAVÂHANA *with the nectar of immortality.*

Arise!
Jîmûtavâhana!

[JÎMÛTAVÂHANA *stands up.*

KING. Receive our praise!
Gaurî divine! it is to thee we owe

Our son! He lives again.

QUEEN. By Gaurî's aid!

[JÎMÛTAVÂHANA, *seeing* GAURÎ, *puts his hands together.*

JÎMÛT. O, how could thy divine assistance fail!
Thou givest all we ask! Thou tak'st away
Pain from thy worshippers! Low at thy feet
I fall, O my protectress: hymns of praise
Shall rise to thee from the Vidyâdharas.

[*Shower of nectar falls.*

KING. Ah! tell me! What is this? I see no cloud!

GAURÎ. The gods, in answer to Garuḍa's prayer,
Have sent the rain of immortality.
For he, repentant, would restore to life
Thy son, and all the Nâga chiefs whose bones
Lie here in whitening heaps. Dost thou not see,
O King! the Nâga lords: their jewel crests
Sparkling upon their heads: they lick the earth
With forked tongues, in eagerness to gain
Their share of the immortal shower that falls:
And then, with forms restored again to life,
In all their pristine beauty, see they glide
With winding course under the ocean wave
Ev'n as a rushing river.
(*Addresses* JÎMÛTAVÂHANA) O my son!
The gift of life alone is not enough
For such as thou! my blessing must be thine
In fuller measure! Thee I consecrate

With sacred water, by my power and will,
Brought from Lake Mânasa in jewelled urns—
Water all golden with the dust that falls,
Shaken from lotus flow'rs by swans, that glide
Upon the bosom of the lake: with this
Here, at this moment do I consecrate
Thee lord and king of the Vidyâdharas:
To thee I give, marked out in gold and gems,
The mystic sign: to thee the elephant
With four white tusks: to thee this charger black:
To thee I give thy bride. Most noble king!
Lord of the universe! to thee I give
These jewelled offerings. O see, the lords
Of the Vidyâdharas, who humbly come
Before thy presence: in their hands they bear
The royal fans, white as the autumn moon,
And as they bow in homage at thy feet,
Their flashing gems send forth a rainbow light,
Matanga at their head, thine enemy!
All this is thine! Tell me what further boon
I may bestow on thee?

JÎMÛT. What shall I ask?
The life of Śankhachûda has been saved:
Garuḍa has been brought to penitence,
The Nâga lords have been restored to life:
My parents live, receiving me again
From death:

I have been made the sovereign lord
Of all the world: and thou hast shown thyself
To me in human form! What can I ask?
Yet in the sage's words: O may the clouds

Send down from heav'n the seasonable shower,
Making the peacocks dance with joy: the
earth,
Clothéd with verdure as a robe, bring forth
Her plenteous harvest; may the nations keep
High festival, rejoicing with their friends
In song and dance, from all misfortune free,
Of merit laying up abundant store,
By envy or by hate, untouched their minds.
[*Exeunt.*

END OF ACT V

NOTES

NOTES ON THE CHARACTERS

Vidyâdharas = possessors of wisdom, are represented as a class of inferior deities inhabiting the regions between earth and sky. They are attendants upon India, but have kings and chiefs of their own, and are represented as intermarrying and having intercourse with men (Dowson, Class. Dict. Hindu Myth.); cf. Gen. 6. 2. " The sons of God saw the daughters of men that they were fair ; and they took them wives of all that they chose." Sons of God, being explained as meaning in the original, " belonging to the class of supernatural beings."

Siddhas = perfected. A class of semi-divine b ings possessing supernatural power, but like the last mentioned associated with men.

Nâga = a serpent. Mythical personages with the head of a cobra. In Act V, Scene 2, the Nâga Prince describes the serpent appearance as the proof of Nâga identity ; — the scales — the double tongues — the triple hood. They were supposed to inhabit Pâtâla, a region below the earth. A race of Nâgas really existed, who have left behind them various evidences of their existence. They are supposed to have been a race distinct from the Hindûs, and to have been called Nâgas from the fact that serpents were an object of worship. Nâgpur = City of the Serpent, owes its name to them. The reader may be referred to the mysterious and not easily explained story of the Serpent in the Wilderness, an object of Sacramental Worship.

Garuḍa = a mythical being, half man, half eagle. He is represented as the King of the Birds, and the great enemy of the serpents. He has a vast number of designations, under which he is known.

Âtreya = the Brâhman. Called also the Vidûshaka. This character always appears in dramatic works, as the confidant, and attendant of the hero. Vidûshaka = buffoon—and his part corresponds something to the "fool" of mediæval society. Although the character is one of a low (somewhat vulgar) description, and the personator is represented as a glutton, and a drunkard, and perhaps worse: he is always represented as a Brâhman, and belonging to a higher caste than the King, or Prince, whose companion he is. The Brâhman had from his birth, and in consequence of his birth, supernatural powers, and a religious position above ordinary people; so that the position of the Vidûshaka may be paralleled by a Priest or Levite among the Jews being brought forward on the stage and made a butt of for his follies or vices. For something similar to the treatment of the Brâhman, one might compare Boccaccio's "Decameron," where any crimes or offences of unusual enormity are attributed to Priests or Monks and Nuns, or

Anchorites. Perhaps the Brâhmanical caste had such a hold over the minds and imaginations of men, that their being made a subject of ridicule was a matter of no consequence.

NOTES ON THE TEXT

Page 23, line 1. The Nândî or Benediction is unique, in being addressed to Buddha. Every Hindû drama has a benedictory introduction, the object being Siva, the popular Hindû deity. This Nândî contains an account of the way in which Buddha was assailed by a certain deity named Mâra, equivalent to Kâma (the Hindû Cupid). Mâra, according to Buddhist theology, means devil, or evil spirit. Mâra is said to have attempted to divert Buddha in his meditations by legions of demons: this being unsuccessful he sent his fascinating daughters. The Buddha, however, was not to be taken in by their wiles, and sent them away with a severe rebuke for trying to hinder his spiritual progress. This legend may be paralleled by the stories about St. Anthony, as well as other Saints. The moral is the same in both cases—that the tempter is most dangerous in the form of an Angel of light.

p. 23, l. 7. "The enlightened one—the conqueror," in the original, Buddhojinah = Buddha, the overcomer of all things, a generic term applied to a Buddha or chief Saint of the Sect (M. Wilhâm. lex.). Buddha, it should be explained, perhaps, is not a name but a title.

The name of *the* Buddha was Śâkya-muni, or Śâkya-simha. He has a real existence, being born at Kapila-Vastu. His father Suddhoduna, of the family of the Śâkyas, was king of the country, and his mother Mâyâdevi of royal parentage. He therefore belonged to the Kshatriya caste. Another name—Gautama (by which he is known), comes from the race to which his family belonged, and Buddha—which means the "Enlightened One," or one who has a perfect knowledge of the truth, was given in later times. He is known by a variety of names and epithets.

p. 24, l. 1. "While Indra gazed," etc. Literally—"Indra looking on with his hair standing on end with astonishment." It ought to be remarked, that Indra is represented as taking an interest (and perhaps something more) in the scene of the Buddha's temptation, since the gods of Hindû mythology are said to be jealous of the austerities practised by men, by means of which humanity is raised to the divine level. Probably, therefore, the idea lying behind is, that Mâra, or Kâma, was put on to tempt Buddha by the gods.

p. 26, l. 12. "Malaya's Hill." This is a range of mountains in Malabar, the Western Ghats in the Dekkan. The mountains abound in sandal trees. The sights and scents of this garden-like district fill Jîmûtavâhana with misgiving, lest his mind may be distracted from the path of devotion which he has marked out.

p. 27, l. 28. "The mysteries of sacred lore,"

refer to the learning and explanation of the Vedas, performed respectively by the disciples and sages.

p. 33, l. 6. "My lord and master Kauśika." The title given to Kauśika is Kula-pati = head or chief of the family. It is explained as one who feeds and teaches 10,000 pupils.

p. 33, l. 10. "The mystic sign." Chakra, explained by M. Wilhâm (lex.) as a circle or depression of the body for mystical, astrological, or cheiromantic purposes. Jîmûtavâhana appears to have had the mark, a mark of sovereignty, on the soles of his feet.

p. 37, l. 15. "Lord of the darts whose tips are armed with flowers!" Kâma, the Hindû Erôs, is armed with a bow and arrows. The bow is of sugar-cane, the bow-string is a line of bees and each arrow is tipped with a flower.

p. 40, l. 1. "Have I not gazed," etc. To a person in the condition of Jîmûtavâhana, it should be explained that all these things are absolutely painful.

p. 40, l. 21. "The moonstone slab." This is a kind of crystal, said to exude moisture under the moon's influence.

p. 47, l. 22. "From which the moon sprang forth." The moon was supposed to have sprung forth from the ocean when the gods churned it up for the ambrosia.

p. 48, l. 13. "Marriage according to the Gandharva rites." Gandharva marriage is one of the eight forms of marriage described, Manu. iij. 6. "Mutual contract based on affection is declared to be lawful for Kshatriyas." This form of marriage is founded on affection, without consent of parents or any ceremonial (cf. what are termed 'Scotch marriages').

p. 50, l. 21. In these words there is an untranslatable pun. Sékharaka, the name of this hanger-on = a garland. Navamâlikâ, the girl's name = Jasmine.

p. 53, l. 3. "The sacred thread." The peculiar thread worn by the first three of the sacred castes—Brâhmans, Kshatriyas, and Vaiśyas: a cord hanging diagonally over the body, from the left shoulder to the right hip.

p. 63, l. 1. There are several words in this speech which have a double meaning, untranslatable in English. The chamberlain—ruler of the Seraglio—bears, a staff, "daṇḍa," as a king bears a sceptre: he looks after the "antahpura," inner chambers, as the king looks after the inner government of cities. "Skhalan," the faults and mistakes (trippings) in the State, corrected by the king; in the ladies' apartments, by the chamberlain.

p. 71, l. 17. "Viśvâmitra . . . took dog's flesh." "He who, to save his life takes food, wherever it may have come from, is not defiled thereby. . . . Viśvâmitra, the discerning between right and wrong, when he was overcome by hunger, took the leg of a dog from a Chandâla's hand and ate it." (Manu. x. 108. Cf. 1 Sam. 21. 6.)

p. 78, l. 6. "Of Jîmûtavâhana." Depends on something said by the messenger behind the scene, and is spoken as he comes on. In its connection with the king's last words it is an expression of evil omen.

p. 86, l. 3. "How canst thou doubt?" Śankhachuda gives in detail the signs by which the Nâgas may be distinguished from men. A learned Hindû, in an interesting article in the "Indian Antiquary," thinks that the Hindû account of the Creation preserves traces of the Revelation in Genesis, which represents the Spirit as "brooding over the face of the waters": and that the Nâgas, half serpents, half men, whose abode was Pâtâla (the lower regions), is a confirmation of the account of the appearance, described in Genesis, of the Serpent to Adam and Eve, and of the conversation he held with them. He suggests (ingeniously enough) that the 'Serpent' was a species of Nâga, in semi-human form, before the curse was pronounced upon him, whereby he was obliged to "go upon his belly and eat dust."

p. 97, l. 2. "Brought from Lake Mânasa." There is a play of words here totally untranslatable. Mânasa is the name of a lake, and also means "conceived in the mind." Therefore the word implies, "water evolved from the inner consciousness of Gaurî, as efficacious for consecrating *as if* it had come from Lake Mânasa."

WILLIAM BRENDON AND SON, LTD. PRINTERS, PLYMOUTH